MARINE
FORCE RECON

MBI

This edition first published in 2003 by
MBI Publishing Company, Galtier Plaza, Suite 200,
380 Jackson Street, St. Paul, MN 55101-3885 USA

MBI Publishing Company titles are also available at
discounts in bulk quantity for industrial or sales-
promotional use. For details write to Special Sales
Manager at Motorbooks International Wholesalers &
Distributors, Galtier Plaza, Suite 200, 380 Jackson
Street, St. Paul, MN 55101-3885 USA.

Library of Congress Cataloging-in-Publication Data

Pushies, Fred J.
    Marine Force Recon / by Fred J. Pushies.
        p. cm.
    ISBN 0-7603-1011-4 (pbk. : alk. paper)
        1. United States. Marine Corps--Commando troops.
        2. Reconnaissance operations. I. Title.

VE23.P87 2003
359.9'6413'0973--dc21

On the Front Cover: Reconnaissance and
surveillance is the "Green Side" of Force Recon
missions. Here, a Recon Marine is using a pair of M19
binoculars.

On the Title Page: The Marines of Force Recon are
an integral part of the MAGTF, operating as a
reconnaissance asset or element of the Maritime
Special Purpose Force (MSPF).

On the Back Cover: A CH-46 Sea Knight helicopter
lifts a team of Force Recon Marines off the ground
during training of the Special Patrol
Insertion/Extraction (SPIE) rig. *Defense Visual
Information Center*

About the Author: Fred Pushies has spent the last 15
years in the company of each of unit assigned to
United States Special Operations Command (SOCOM).
Fred has traveled extensively as a photographer and
writer, from the mountains of the Rangers' training
camp, to the desert with Special Forces mobility
teams—the same teams who are now active in the
Iraqi wasteland.

Fred has spend countless hours in Air Force Special
Operations Command (AFSOC) Spectre gunships and
Pave Low helicopters, as well as flying at treetop level
with the 160th Special Operations Aviation Regiment.
He has skimmed across the waves with the SEALs in a
Mark V and crunched through the brush with Force
Recon Marines. Fred's integrity and insight are evident
in his previous works: *US Air Force Special Ops, US Army
Special Forces*, and the upcoming *Special Ops: America's
Elite Forces in 21st Century Combat*.

Edited by Steve Gansen
Designed by LeAnn Kuhlmann

Printed in China

Contents

Foreword

Marines have long recognized that our Corps' continued success depends on our willingness and ability to prepare for and adapt to ever-evolving national security challenges and opportunities around the globe. As a force in readiness, the Marine Corps, in close partnership with the Navy, is proud of its contributions to America's forward presence and expeditionary force projection capabilities. At the heart of our Corps' war fighting prowess are the skills of Marine riflemen, and nowhere is this in greater evidence than among Force Reconnaissance Marines.

The Force Reconnaissance Marines of the United States Marine Corps are the warriors the Corps looks to when the mission requires special stealth and precision. From deep reconnaissance missions to the control of supporting arms and direct action missions, Force Recon Marines are tasked with some of the Corps' most demanding and dangerous missions. Fred Pushies' *Marine Force Recon* depicts the special skills of Force Reconnaissance Marines and illustrates how their spirit and training combine to give them their unique capabilities.

For members of the Corps' family as well as those who wish to better understand Marine Force Recon, Fred Pushies' *Marine Force Recon* is a valuable resource. In addition to being a remarkable photographic documentary, this finely researched volume provides both a history and a survey of the Corps' reconnaissance units—including the selection, training, equipment, tactics, and techniques of our Recon Marines.

Fred Pushies' excellent work is a superb celebration of Force Recon Marines—both those who have served in the past and those who serve today. His photos capture the essence of these elite warriors.

—James L. Jones
General, U.S. Marine Corps

Acknowledgments

I begin by thanking God for His blessing over our great nation, with the hope He will continue to hold us and our cause in the hollow of His hand. To those who have gone before, and those who are currently making the great sacrifice on the altar of freedom, my profound thanks. For my wife Tammy, who held down the home front while I was out roaming through the brush with the Marines, and for the support of my family, I am also grateful.

I would like to thank: Gunnery Sergeant Joseph Zimmerman and Lance Corporal J. Parsons, both USMC Recruiters, and Captain Heil, USMC PAO-NY, for starting me on my trip into the world of the United States Marines.

My editors, Sara Perfetti and Steve Gansen, MBI Publishing Company, for their guidance.

At HQ USMC: Commandant of the Marine Corps General James L. Jones, Major Jeffery S. Kojac, and Gunnery Sergeant Anita L. Standage.

PAO-Camp Lejeune: Captain Nick Ritzcovan, Lieutenant Kelly Frushour, Lieutenant Marisol Cantu; PAO-26th MEU(SOC): Captain James Jarvis, Gunnery Sergeant Mark Bradley, Lance Corporal Marcus Miller, Lance Corporal Rathal Willis; PAO-Camp Pendleton: Lieutenant Tara Burkhart; Navy Chief Information Office: Lieutenant Commander David Waterman; Bureau of Medicine and Surgery, New York: Lieutenant Junior Grade Mike Kafka, deputy public affairs officer.

Amphibious Reconnaissance School, Fort Story: Major Chris Medlin OIC, Major D.S. Howe, Staff Sergeant Rob Salter, Gunnery Sergeant Brian T. Foy (SNCOIC), Staff Sergeant William McFarland, Sergeant Chadwick Carson, Staff Sergeant Joe Weirsky; Members of Class 03-02 Team One: Captain Rick Bernier, Corporal David Sigler, Corporal John Avak, Corporal Matthew Martin, Lance Corporal Joel Wood, Lance Corporal Juan Chavez, Private First Class Amos Savell, Private First Class Branden Earhart; Members of Class / 03-02 Team Two: First Lieutenant Tad Douglas, Sergeant Jon Balkowitsch, Corporal Michael Brunmeier, Lance Corporal Donny Patel, Lance Corporal Isaac Meraz; Basic Reconnaissance Course, Coronado, California: Private First Class Broch Hileman, Staff Sergeant Archer.

USMC Museum, Navy Yard: Colonel John Ripley (ret.), Lena Kaljot, Ed Finney; National Archives, Washington, D.C.: Sharon Culley; MCCDC, Doctrine Division, Quantico, Virginia: Lieutenant Colonel Pat Redman; U.S. Army Combined Arms Doctrine Directorate: Lieutenant Colonel Patrick Ryan; Defense Visual Information Center: Kathy Vinson; Marine Corps Association, *Marine Corps Gazette* and *Leatherneck Magazine*: Colonel Walter G. Ford (ret.), Patty Everett; Lieutenant Colonel Robert J. Coates, Bob Buda, and Pat Rogers; Major John DiPietro, deputy chief of police, Miami Township, Ohio.

Thanks to Force Recon Association, their officers and members for a wealth of historical information and for allowing me to participate in their reunion: Dick Sasser, president, Chuck Asher, communications chief, Colonel Bruce Meyers (ret.), Brigadier General Russell Corey (ret.), Allan Bierlein, Duane Neary, James W. "Sam" Sandoz, Lou Kern, Terry Addis, Tom Wilson, Don Griffith, Greg Baxter, Jesse Richburg, Orest Bishko, Pete "Willie" Monroe, J. Marshall "Mac" McKee, Andrew Earl, Colonel Bill Floyd (ret.), Sergeant Major J.A. Kuiken, Brian Deatrick, Charles Buchholz; George Alexander, Hendrik C. "Bruno" Brunsveld, Jim Hill, Major Len DeFrancisci, Mike Schatz, Nick Banno, Reuben

Darby, Tim Lamontagne, Tom Scaringe, Steve "Doc" Andrews, Rick "Rabbi" Rabenold, Gunnery Sergeant Wesley R. Johnson (ret.), and Daniel J. Sullivan. I wish there was enough room to include all the stories, experiences, and photos they shared with me. It was definitely a difficult task choosing what to include.

At Marine Corps System Command, Quantico, Virginia: Major Robert McCarthy, Deputy Project Manger Raids & Recon, Captain Chris Doyle (IFAV), Capt Jerome Bryant (Weapons), Gunnery Sergeant David E. Grandin, small craft project officer, and Gunnery Sergeant Robert Perry.

John Jones, ACR Electronics; Steve Siderias, Extreme Outfitters; Gene Higdon, High Speed Gear; Rick Scriven, vice-president, Zodiac of North America.

Colonel Andrew P. Frick, Commanding Officer 26th Marine Expeditionary Force (Special Operations Capable).

Staff Sergeant Gregory Funk, PAO New River; Gunnery Sergeant Mark Bell and Sergeant Michael Michaelson, VMMT-204 MV-22 Osprey Program; Staff Sergeant Robert Blanton RIP Sergeant; Staff Sergeant David Lind, 2nd Platoon, 1st Force Reconnaissance Company, Camp Pendleton, California.

Special thanks to Staff Sergeant Joe Tablada for his assistance, and his 1st Platoon, 4th Force Reconnaissance Company, including Corporal Frank Prinea III, Corporal William P. Heiman, Corporal Jake Pazienza, and Corporal Jared "JD" McAfee. Also, Staff Sergeant Marty Rademacher, Ops Chief, 4th Force Recon.

At 2nd Force Reconnaissance Company, Camp Lejeune, North Carolina: Lieutenant Colonel Jim Reilly III, commanding officer, Major Oliver B. Spencer (XO), Major Demetrius F. Maxey (S-3), Major Jeff C. Evans, Major David Falk, Sergeant Major William Bly, Master Sergeant C. S. Boyd, Gunnery Sergeant Rod J. Guyton, Gunnery Sergeant Bill Schanz, Staff Sergeant William "Plug" Daniels, Staff Sergeant Michael Glauner, Sergeant Jonathan Brown, Sergeant Carlos Snead, Sergeant Matthew Rackley, Sergeant Ryan Alton, Sergeant Jason Quinn, HMCS Michael Munn, and EN2 Frank Lasch; 5th Platoon, 2nd Force Reconnaissance Company, Camp Lejeune, North Carolina: Gunnery Sergeant Tim Hatcher, Staff Sergeant Derek Lovell, and Sergeant Steven Little.

I am extremely grateful to Captain Andy Christian and Gunnery Sergeant Edward Lynch for their insight, direction and assistance; their help was indispensable in this project. Captain Christian is the commanding officer of 6th Platoon 2nd Force Recon Company Camp Lejeune, North Carolina, and Gunnery Sergeant Lynch is the platoon sergeant. I would like to thank the Marines of 6th Platoon, 2nd Force Reconnaissance Company for their time, information, and camaraderie during my many visits; it is greatly appreciated. My thanks to: Staff Sergeant Cody Able, Staff Sergeant Robbie Achee, Staff Sergeant Kenneth Forbes, Staff Sergeant Javier Obleas, Staff Sergeant Macky Outlaw, Staff Sergeant Charlie Cox, Staff Sergeant Frank Parker, Sergeant Travis Haley, Sergeant Bryan Maas, Sergeant Keith Perrigon, Sergeant Patrick Cotter, Sergeant Stephen Bellville, Sergeant Ross Brady, Sergeant Xavier Lendoff, Sergeant Sean Mickle, Sergeant Richard Hoeltage, Sergeant Brain Pavlus, Sergeant Eric Schera, Sergeant Ronald Wilbanks, and Corporal Mason.

Introduction

Positioned in a cleft in the mountains of Afghanistan, Sergeant Newman silently pulls the drawstrings of his Gore-Tex parka a little tighter, in response to the wintry blast. He glances over at his teammate, Sergeant Jimenez, who is lying an arm's length away. Jimenez is surveying the enemy's position approximately 2,000 meters away. The young Marine shifts his attention slightly to his left as the team leader, Gunnery Sergeant Thomas, quietly edges over next to Sergeant Jimenez. The movements of the veteran Force Reconnaissance Marine are deliberate and so exact, they are barely audible in the wind swept boulders of the harbor site.

The Gunny stops his crawl just short of the mountainous parapet where Sergeant Jimenez is positioned. The Marine shifts his gaze toward his newly arrived teammate; using his index and middle fingers formed as a "V," he points to his eyes. Then with the fingers together, he points to the enemy compound. Again, using hand signals, he indicates that three convoys of SUVs and trucks have entered the suspected Al Qaeda compound.

Gunnery Sergeant Thomas glances toward the compound, then at Sergeant Jimenez, giving him a "thumbs up" as he egresses from the earthwork boundary and down to the radio. As he approaches a small rift in the rocks, he mimes the sign of a telephone handset to the "comm" Sergeant, who in turn reaches over and picks up the H-250 handset and passes it over to the Gunny.

Following the team's SOP, Gunnery Sergeant Thomas reports: suspect target is on-site. Through the use of short code words, he conveys the enemy's strength, positions, and weapons, including any ground-to-air threats, from Stinger missiles or RPGs. Thomas passes the handset back to his comm man and once again moves up to Jimenez.

By the time the Gunny reaches the rock ledge, Sergeant Jimenez has set up the SIDS camera and has begun to capture the enemy's movements digitally as they unfold before him. The data is then uplinked via SatCom back to Camp Hippo and the commander of the Marine Expeditionary Unit (Special Operations Capable), or MEU(SOC). The commander views the compound, and a short while later Marine helicopters filled with combat-laden warriors begin to lift skyward and toward the enemy compound.

As Gunny Thomas signals to his team to start packing, a Marine F/A-18 Hornet screams over their position; moments later the pilot releases the GLB-82 smart bomb slung beneath its wing. The terminally guided ordnance hones in on the target with deadly accuracy; a result of a second Force Recon team "painting" the barracks building in the compound with an AN/PEQ-1A SOFLAM laser designator. As the explosion echoes through the mountains, all that is left of the building is a smoking bomb crater.

As the explosive dust settles on the Afghan ground, over the horizon a group of CH-46 Sea Knight helicopters loaded with Marines appears and closes in on the target area. The helicopters arrive, mixing the dust of the ground with the debris of the target, and troops disgorge themselves from the rotary craft to engage the enemy.

As the Sea Knights begin their return trip to the base, two helicopters peel off from the formation. One will extract Gunnery Sergeant Thomas and his team, while the other will pick up the "Targeting" team. Having spent the last four days in the mountains, the men have accomplished their objective and now head back to base to await their next mission.

The above scenario is an example of a Deep Recon and Direct Action mission carried out by the men of the U.S. Marine Corps Force Reconnaissance. As the American population discovered on 11 September 2001, the most powerful nation in the world can become a target if one item of information is lacking. The most lethal military force on any battlefield can never hope to achieve victory if this data is not available to its commander. This precious commodity is called *intelligence*. For this purpose, the United States Marine Corp employs a group of highly trained, experienced, and dedicated warriors skilled in the discipline of reconnaissance. Knowing who, what, when, where, and how the enemy is going to attack can make the difference between victory and defeat.

A leader once said, "If I would have my way, I should have two armies: One, which would present itself in colors, precision drilling, and parade. The other would be comprised of warriors, who would be skilled in the art of war, and those would be the ones I should send into battle." Such a group is already in existence: the United States Marine Corps. From the Silent Drill Team, the United States Marine Band known as "The Presidents' Own," and the U.S. Marine Drum and Bugle Corp called "The Commandants' Own," there is not a unit in the U.S. military with a presence more dignified and elegant than the U.S. Marines. The Corps is also the home of the most ferocious, dedicated, and lethal warriors in the U.S. arsenal of democracy, referred to as "The Nation's Finest."

The Marine Corps in itself constitutes an "elite" military force; self-sufficient and highly capable to engage in any mission given, anytime and anywhere. As we look at Marine Force Reconnaissance, we are confronted with a quandary; in fact, Force Recon Marines are an "elite" within an "Elite." There are those in the Corps, both veteran and active Marines, who espouse this assessment, while others eschew the perception. Without a doubt, it is an indisputable fact the Marines produce some of the finest riflemen in the military: from cook to pilot, every Marine is first and foremost a rifleman. Regarding esprit de corps, talk with members of a Marine Infantry Rifle Company and they'll tell you they are superior to the folks in supply. Have a conversation with the pilots and they will tell you the Harrier pilots are a cut above the Hornet drivers; and so it goes. In my observation, the U.S. Marine Corps is a spear with a shaft, binding, and spearhead, each entity working together as one to strike at the heart of any foe of freedom. Without hesitation it can be acknowledged that the Marines of Force Recon are indeed the tip of that spear.

CHAPTER 1

History

The lineage of today's Force Recon Marines can be traced as far back as 1906, when a formal doctrine was written on American Amphibious Reconnaissance. Prior to World War II a publication referred to as FTP-167 Landing Operations Doctrine was produced, which covered scouting of landing sites. In a Fleet Exercise called FLEX4, which ran from January through March of 1938, Marines put to the test the doctrine set forth in FTP-167. For this exercise, the 5th Marine Regiment provided troops to act as recon teams. Following subsequent Fleet Exercises, an "Observer Group" was created in 1942, consisting of two officers and 20 enlisted provided from the First Marine Division. This Marine OG would be the first unit trained in Amphibious Reconnaissance.

On 7 January 1943, the Observer Group was re-designated the Amphibious Reconnaissance Company (ARC) under the command of Captain James L. Jones. In the summer of 1943, the Amphibious Corps would be reorganized and the ARC would become "Amphibious Reconnaissance Company, V Amphibious Company," or ARC (VAC). They would participate in operations in the Apamama, Majuro, and Eniwetok atoll islands. The V Amphibious Corps Reconnaissance Company was assigned to pinpoint the location of the enemy throughout the atolls. The ARC would undergo an evolution when on 14 April 1944 it would become the Amphibious Reconnaissance Battalion with a complement of 20 officers, 270 enlisted men, and 13 Navy Corpsmen. Worth noting is that simultaneously, Marines were attached to the "Coast Watcher" units; recon teams from "Special Service Unit Number 1" served the forces in the southwest Pacific.

A pivotal moment for the Reconnaissance Marines would come in July 1944 in the assault on Tinian Island. The turf war between the Marines and Navy arose when Lieutenant General Holland Smith and Vice Admiral Kelly Turner disagreed on the proposed landing site. As Colonel Bruce Meyers (ret.) explains, "The question revolves around who makes the ultimate decision on the landing site. Is it the ground unit that is going to have to cross a particular beach, or is it the navy type who must bring the Marines to the site and then support them with supplies and with naval gunfire and air support?" To put an end to the dispute, the Recon Marines were tasked with surveying both sites. Armed with only Ka-Bar knives, the Marines of the Amphibious Reconnaissance Company, VAC carried out their mission. Brigadier General Russell Corey (ret.) relates, "There were two landings sites, White 2 and White 1. The beaches were about 60 yards and 160 yards (wide) respectively. (Corey) and Gunny Charles Patrick led the two recon teams. The first night the current was so strong we could only conduct the recon on one of the beaches. The next night we returned and were able to do both landing sites." Upon the returning with their findings; the site choice went to Lieutenant General Smith, and beaches White 1 and White 2 were chosen for the landing of two divisions of Marines on Tinian. Brigadier General Corey adds, "Had the division gone ashore on the spot picked by Kelly, it would have been a slaughter. The Japs had gun emplacements and artillery all lined up in the Tinian Town location." The Recon Marines had earned their pay, and would see subsequent service in Iwo Jima and Okinawa, as well as other amphibious assaults in the Pacific.

During this time it would become a common sight to see U.S. Marines training alongside of Navy Underwater Demolition Teams (UDT) at Fort Pierce, Florida. Here they would learn skills in hydrographic survey, cast & recover, free diving, and demolitions, to name just a few. During World War II there would be over 108 amphibious reconnaissance missions carried out by this select group of Marines, often equipped

U.S. Marines of the 1st Marine Division Reconnaissance Company make the first helicopter landing on Hill 812, Korea, 20 September 1951. The Marines are credited with being the first service ever to deploy combat troops via helicopter. From Korea to Afghanistan the helicopter has served as a primary insertion platform for the Recon Marines. *National Archive*

with merely swim gear, coral shoes, and a Ka-Bar knife with which to accomplish their missions.

After World War II, in 1948 the Corps continued to explore and experiment with the reconnaissance activity. A Recon Company was created from D Co., 5th Marine Regiment, commanded by Captain Kenneth J. Houghton. At the onset of the Korean War, Captain Ken Houghton and his Marines would trade in their recon exercises for actual combat. According to General Houghton (ret.), "We did primarily ground reconnaissance behind enemy lines. This would be approximately five miles in front of the Regiment. The majority of patrolling was done on foot with the occasional use of jeeps. We would use two or three jeeps armed with .50-cal machine guns." The recon Marines would be merged into the parent organization, the 1st Marine Division, to become the 1st Marine Division Reconnaissance Company.

On 1 December 1950, 2nd Amphibious Reconnaissance Battalion was activated at Camp Lejeune, North Carolina, under the command of Major Regan Fuller. It was subsequently reduced to company strength on 11 August 1952. While on the West Coast at Camp Pendleton, the 1st Amphibious Reconnaissance Platoon was formed on 12 March 1951. During the Korean War there would be two Amphibious Reconnaissance units active, the 1st Amphibious Recon Company operating from the West Coast and the 2nd Amphibious Recon Company operating on the East Coast. During this time, there were occasions when the Recon Marines would work with Navy Underwater Demolition Teams (UDT) conducting raids into the North.

Following the stalemate of the Korean War, the Marines went on training, this time for the unthinkable. During the escalation of the Cold War in the mid-1950s, they planned their operations for a nuclear battlefield and adjusted techniques and procedures accordingly. The Marine Corps directed the creation of Marine Corps Test Unit Number 1 on 1 July 1954 at Camp Pendleton, to develop new battle plans using the helicopter as the primary method of insertion.

While World War II Marines assaulted sandy beachheads, the nuclear era would find them assaulting not beach heads, but rather air heads hundreds of miles inland. From the efforts of MTCU#1 it became clear that heliborne assaults would necessitate intelligence that could only be derived from deep reconnaissance, details such as scouting Landing Zones in areas of enemy concentration. Subsequently, a year later, on 12 May 1955, Reconnaissance Platoon MCTU#1 was formed. The new commander, Captain Joseph Z. Taylor, was given extensive leeway to adapt, overcome, and improvise tactics to exploit the capabilities needed to wage war in an expanded battlefield

Among these potential proposals was the use of helicopters for vertical deployment of troops and for insertion of reconnaissance teams. Helicopters had proved extremely useful in Korea and thus were on the forefront of possibilities to expand the Marines' missions. While the rotary aircraft had definite advantages in the ability to leapfrog over the adversary and deliver recon teams deep behind enemy lines, they also had disadvantages. The helicopters were easy to detect and limited in range and in their ability to fly at night and during inclement weather. In addition to these restrictions, the helicopters could be finicky machines, and vulnerable to ground fire—a fact confirmed decades later at Desert One in Iran and in Mogadishu, Somalia.

As an alternative to helicopters, the option of airborne insertion via parachute was introduced by a number of Recon officers. Colonel Meyers, already having jumped with the Navy, brought this and pathfinding issues to Lieutenant General Lewis B. "Chesty" Puller. Colonel Meyers relates, "I did a draft letter for the CMC (Commandant of the Marine Corps) and Chesty signed it." With

Combat equipped members of the Marine Force Reconnaissance Company prepare to move out in the IBS (Inflatable Boat, Small) from the *USS Greenfish* for the infiltration of an "enemy held" beach. From World War II to today, the Marines have been capable of operating with submarines as an insertion platform. *National Archive*

the blessing of the Commandant Marine Corps and Puller, Taylor and Meyers would organize the Parachute Reconnaissance/Parachute Pathfinder Project. Consequently, the Recon Platoon packed their gear and in April of 1956 headed off to Ft. Benning, Georgia, to undergo training at the U.S. Army Airborne School. Upon graduation, the Marines were awarded their Silver Wings, or "Elks Tooth" as they were often called. A handful of the Recon Marines would remain at Ft. Benning to attend the Army Jumpmaster Course.

Worth noting is the fact that these Marines, who would forge the path that future Force Recon

"The New Breed," an eleven-man parachute pathfinder team, displays the equipment it carries for one of the Leathernecks' parachute missions. The equipment, which includes radios, helicopter guide panels, smoke signals, and lights for night landing, averages between fifty and ninety pounds per man. The prime mission of the unit is to guide helicopter-borne assault forces into landing sites and then assist assault troops in movement from the landing zone. *National Archive*

A Marine Corps four-man parachute scout team poses with a portion of their gear necessary to accomplish their mission. Well-versed in the art of surviving off the land, the team will carry only a minimum food supply. Special radio equipment with which to communicate with high-flying aircraft was just being tested in January 1958. *National Archive*

Marines would follow, received their parachute training at the U.S. Navy Test Parachutist course run by CWO Lew Vinson, USN, at El Centro. It was the Recon Marines who were the first U.S. combat forces to employ free-fall parachuting techniques as a method of insertion. Honing these skills, the Marines were practicing parachute insertion from almost anything the Navy had in the air. Such jumps would include those made from carrier-based jet aircraft called "the coal chute." Colonel Meyers comments, ". . . (T)he jumper slides down the chute ([in the F3D Skyknight) or as in the A3D Skywarrior out the bomb bay." He adds, "This was without any bail out bottles (of oxygen)."

Force Reconnaissance as it is known today was activated on 19 June 1957 with the creation of 1st Amphibious Reconnaissance Company FMFPAC (Fleet Marine Force Pacific) under the command of Major Bruce F. Meyers. Located at Camp Pendleton, California, this new company would be formed into three platoons: Amphibious Reconnaissance Platoon, Parachute Reconnaissance Platoon, and Pathfinder Reconnaissance Platoon. Subsequently, in 1958 half of the company was transferred from Camp Pendleton to Camp Lejeune, to form the 2nd Force Reconnaissance Company FMFLANT (Fleet Marine Force Atlantic) under the command of Captain Joe Taylor and supporting the 2nd

A five-man amphibious reconnaissance team kneels with a nylon boat and equipment necessary for their mission, 20 January 1958. Equipment includes aqua-lungs, depth gauges, wrist compasses, and exposure suits which enable swimmers to work in extremely cold water. All members of the team are outstanding swimmers, capable of breasting high surf and rough waters. *National Archive*

Marine Division. Worth noting is the fact that it would be another four years before the Navy SEALs would come on the scene, and another 11 years before the Army would designate a counterpart to Force Recon with the creation of LRRPs (Long Range Recon Patrols).

As the country progressed into a new decade, the Marines of Force Recon also advance in their tactics, techniques, and procedures. These men, proficient in land navigation, small arms tactics, and patrolling, and having earned their wings, would now depart from terra firma to master the skills of attacking from the sea. Fast boats, rubber rafts, and submarines were not new to the Marines, having used these craft as platforms during World War II and Korea. Methods of locking-in and -out of submarines and buoyant ascents would all serve the Force Recon Marines in performing their missions. While the men were honing their skills, the United States was becoming ensconced in the Republic of Vietnam. That tiny country would prove to be a watershed for Marine Force Reconnaissance.

Members of 1st Force Reconnaissance Company would be deployed to Vietnam in 1965. During this time 2nd Force had the assignment of training new Recon Marines to be sent to Southeast Asia. The Force Recon Marines at Lejeune would also serve as the primary unit should any other contingency arise elsewhere that needed the attention of the U.S. Marine Corps. Because of the need for additional reconnaissance capabilities in-country, 3rd Force Company was created. As Lieutenant Colonel Bill Floyd (ret.) recalls, "We took the company over in September of 1965. First would make their home in Dong Ha, while 3rd was in Quang Tri." When the Marines of Force Recon first deployed to Vietnam, they were armed only with M3A1 "Grease Guns." Subsequently, they would migrate to the M-14 and eventually to the M-16 assault rifle.

Marines are taught to fight, to give no quarter, and to defeat the enemy at all costs. Conversely, reconnaissance work required stealth and patience; at times you let the enemy pass by so you can report on their movements. The aggressiveness of the U.S. Marine was something that had to be unlearned in order for reconnaissance to be successful. To enhance these new skills in Force Reconnaissance Companies, many of the Marines attended Recondo School taught by members of the U.S. Army 5th Special Force Group (Airborne).

Recondo, an amalgamation of Reconnaissance/ Commando, taught the Force Recon Marines new techniques and honed time-honored tactics to a razor's edge. Here, among fellow Americans, ROK

Members of Team 3-1, 1st Platoon, 2nd Force Recon Company, Camp Geiger, North Carolina, just prior to deployment to the Republic of Vietnam in July 1967. They are armed with the M-3 .45-caliber "grease guns." *Greg Baxter/Courtesy Jesse Richburg Jr.*

(Republic of Korea), and other allied troops, the men would learn how to rappel from helicopters for insertion and be introduced to the McGuire and STABO rigs to facilitate extraction. The final exam for the class was a "live" insertion and patrol in enemy territory.

During the Vietnam War, two types of missions would weave their way into the tapestry of the Force Recon fabric. These were called "Key Hole" and "Sting Ray" operations. In an article in *Marine Corps Gazette* of May 1969, authors Major General R. G. Davis and Lieutenant J. L. Jones, Jr., defined these two types of reconnais-

sance patrols. Key Hole patrols were based on stealth and secrecy. The purpose was pure reconnaissance, with no overt intent to make contact with enemy force. They operated in small teams in remote areas and were lightly armed, their weaponry being for defensive measures to break contact. Conversely, Sting Ray patrols went out looking for trouble. They were heavily armed, including supplemental weapons with which to maintain a prolonged engagement with the enemy. These teams operated closer in, under the cover of fire base artillery. The Sting Ray patrols of the Vietnam era would be akin today to Direct Action missions. It should also be noted that, while Key Hole missions were planned to avoid enemy contact, more often than not those missions could turn into a Sting Ray in a heartbeat, planned or not!

While pure reconnaissance missions avoided contact with the enemy, there were times when Recon teams were actually within arm's reach of the enemy. This was the case as related by Corporal Allan Bierlein, of 3rd Force Reconnaissance Company, 3rd Reconnaissance Battalion, 3rd Marine Division, under the command of Captain W. F. Snyder at Quang Tri. It was 20 November 1968 when Corporal Bierlein assembled his team and issued the Warning Order that they had a recon mission. For the

Kevin Jones and Jim Podesta, members of 3rd Force Reconnaissance Company, navigate their way through a jungle stream in pursuit of the NVA. They are armed with M-16 rifles, which are camouflaged with "100-mph tape" to break up the outline of the weapon. *Courtesy Terry Addis*

Outside of the ammo bunker in Phu Bai, South Vietnam, are members of 3rd Force Recon team "Tinny," an eight man recon team just prior to heading down to the helicopter for their insertion into the Ashau Valley. Standing, l-r: Welbaum, Kiekendall, "Doc" Montgomery, and Kennedy (team leader). Kneeling, l-r: Cox, Gonzales, and Wilson. Eighth man Winermire took the photo. *Courtesy Tom Wilson*

with the enemy makes the most of cover and movement. The basic principle of the Peel follows: Upon initial contact everyone hits the ground, engaging direct fire into the attacking force. The lead man collapses back through a corridor created by his teammates, who are laying down suppressive fire. Reloading their weapons as the move, they are prepared to hit the ground and provide cover fire as the rest of the team collapses on them.

As the team assembles their equipment, they assure noise discipline will be maintained. Each man puts on all of his gear and will jump up and down a few times; if anything rattles or bangs together it is taped down, or tucked in, or removed. Noise discipline is paramount on a recon mission; silence equates to survival. Using parachute shroud lines, the members have stripped away the inner nylon lines and have threaded the neck chain of their dog tags to eliminate any rubbing. They have also taped their metal dog tags together to further silence them.

On Saturday, 23 November, the four members of Team Football Star begin the day by applying their face paint. No one speaks; each man is immersed in his own thoughts of what the day will bring. Once the metamorphosis is complete, they don their "deuce" gear. Corporal Sandoz shoulders the PRC-25 radio and they head to the helicopter pad. Each man is wearing jungle fatigues in the ERDL (Engineer Research Development Laboratory) pattern, sans BVDs.

They are armed with AR15 assault rifles. Affixed to each weapon are numerous strips of green duct tape to break up the outline of the rifle, and the barrel has been taped over to keep it from getting clogged with dirt. There are no slings on the rifles; in their place is a length of para-cord, secured to the pistol grip with tape. The team is also armed with a 40mm M-79 grenade launcher and their personal choice in knives, predominantly Ka-Bars, attached to the 782 gear upside down, ready for action.

next three days, Team Football Star, consisting of Patrol Leader (PL) Corporal Bierlein, Corporal Jim Sandoz (APL&RTO), Gunnery Sergeant Robert Wilhite, and Private First Class Charles Mocchel prepared for the patrol. Weapons were zeroed, equipment was organized, and immediate action drills, or IADs, were practiced.

One of the IADs practiced by the team was the "Peel," better known today as the "Australian Peel." This effective procedure for breaking contact

In addition to the weapons, each man will carry 250 to 300 rounds of 5.56mm ammunition in 20-round magazines, four fragmentation grenades, as well as smoke and CS grenades. Rounding out each man's equipment are a 20-foot length of rope with snap links, poncho liner (but no poncho, too noisy), serum albumin (blood expander), gas mask, and a minimum of two canteens. The team will eat LRRP rations; noise discipline is too important to allow the clicking of a spoon against the C-Rat can, so the peaches stay back at the base. Corporal Bierlein stated that at times, before going into the field, they would bulk up on the C-ration crackers and peanut butter, which "would bind you up for a few days, eliminating waste."

It was time. The four men of Team Football Star approached the rear of the CH-46 Sea Knight helicopter, loading via the rear cargo ramp. The roar of the helicopter engines and the rhythmic beating of the rotor blades would be the last comforting link to friendly forces as the aircraft crossed "over the fence," and into the Hai Lang National Forest in Laos. Upon reaching the insertion point, the pilot brought the Sea Knight to a slight hover a few feet from the ground, and the Force Recon team jumped out. As the helicopter lifted off, the team immediately headed for the relative safety of the tree line, in case there were any enemy "LZ watchers." The pilot would continue on to make two additional "false" insertions, in hopes of throwing off the enemy.

The jungle sounds surrounded the team, and Corporal Bierlein knew they had inserted without being opposed. The patrol was running rather routinely, when on the third day out they observed a large North Vietnamese Army (NVA) column at the bottom of a valley they were overlooking. The enemy had come to their attention because the NVA were blowing bugles at various times of the day. The team established their harbor site and continued to observe the

Corporal Allan Bierlein of 3rd Force Reconnaissance Company prepares to send in a SitRep. Barely visible at the bottom of the handset, which has plastic wrap around it to keep water out, is the shackle card with Code letters and numbers for radio communication. Also, note the application of green "100-mph tape" to his M-16 to further break up the pattern of the weapon. *Courtesy Allan Bierlein*

Reconnaissance Marines display their parachuting and SCUBA equipment, circa 1988. *Defense Visual Information Center*

trap line; from the footprints in the mud it was determined that only one or perhaps two NVA were checking the line. It was assumed the trap line was used to provide food for the NVA encampment. The team headed back toward the top of the hill, where they called in to base. Corporal Bierlein explains, "We intended to extend one additional day and attempt to take a prisoner if things went right."

From their harbor site on the side of the hill, they were in a good position to observe the enemy. There was a wood line and some brush, then the ground opened up for approximately 20 to 30 meters, then more brush. The team was sitting in a tight circle less than three yards in diameter; there was a gap of two or three feet in the brush to accommodate any observations. Bierlein was watching through the gap when he sighted a group of NVA emerging from the brush and into the clearing. They continued to approach and were soon within mere yards of the team's position. The team remained completely motionless; their intent was to let them pass. Bierlein explains, "We've been in that situation before, we were outnumbered, the best thing to do was to let them pass, not initiate any contact." By this time the enemy had the recon team virtually surrounded, but they were passing them without incident. Things were going as well as could be expected, when all of a sudden the NVA squad leader called out and the enemy soldiers came to a halt.

It appeared the enemy patrol was taking a break, as the men began to remove their packs and set their weapons and loads onto the ground. The NVA patrol was right on top of Team Football Star: in fact one of the North Vietnamese soldiers actually sat on Private First Class Mocchel's foot. The Marines held their position, patiently waiting for the enemy to take their break and move on. However, fate would not cooperate with those plans.

area for the next two days. Down on the valley floor could be heard the sound of tracked vehicles moving through the jungle below.

The teams could communicate by prearranged codes with their base using a "shackle" card. This was a plastic card with letters and numbers embossed on it whereby A equaled this number, B equaled that number, and so on. Maintaining strict noise discipline, they would communicate by keying the handset of the PRC-25. Corporal Sandoz, the RTO, would key the handset twice and convey, "Alpha-Sierra," or "all secure." This message would be received by a radio relay station on Hill 950, and forwarded on to base.

On the second day overwatching the trail, the team moved in closer for a better look. On the way back up the hill they noticed a dead fall

The NVA squad leader was casually moving toward the side of the brush were Corporal Bierlein was observing their movements. The enemy soldier took off his pack and leaned forward to set it on the ground. Just as he did so, he turned and looked through the gap in the brush and directly at the Recon Team Patrol Leader. Bierlein relates, "We maintained eye contact for just a second . . . the expression on his face was 'please don't kill me.' I had no option but to initiate contact."

With his AR15 set on full auto, Corporal Bierlein opened fire on the NVA squad leader. As he did so, the rest of the team followed his lead. The first volley of fire by the recon team resulted in several NVA being wounded, as moaning and crying could be heard coming from the bushes and surrounding area. The team directed their automatic fire and grenades at the enemy, and the crying stopped.

Not sure how many NVA were in the area, the team immediately radioed for an extraction. The word came back: there were no air assets available at this time. There was a large troop movement being conducted, and the officer in charge would not release any of his helicopters. The patrol leader got on the PRC-25 and relayed back to camp asking if they wanted the reconnaissance information the team had gathered, or four dead Marines! If they didn't get an extraction helo in fast, they were going to be in serious trouble.

The decision was made to head for the alternate LZ and hope the helicopter would be released by that time. As they started to move out, they threw CS grenades to slow down any pursuing NVA soldiers. This would make it difficult, if not impossible, for any of the wounded to follow, or breathe. The recon team had donned gas masks and was moving through the foliage toward the alternate LZ.

By now the NVA had regrouped and were hunting for the recon patrol. With the NVA

A CH-46 Sea Knight helicopter lifts a team of Force Recon Marines off the ground during training of the Special Patrol Insertion/Extraction (SPIE) rig. Worth noting is that while the Army SF rigs (the McGuire and STABO) are more well known for their use during the Vietnam era, it is the SPIE rig developed by the Marines that is in use with all U.S. SOF units today. *Defense Visual Information Center*

close on their heels, Corporal Bierlein got on the radio and called in an artillery strike; his request was for "danger close." Fortunately for the team, the rounds fell on target, nothing fell short, and the enemy was caught in the lethal rain of inbound artillery rounds. As the team ran for the alternate LZ, shrapnel tore through the air around them.

23

Recon Marines move out on a mission after disembarking from a Marine CH-46E Sea Knight helicopter during Operation Desert Shield. Members of Force Recon performed deep reconnaissance as well as CAS mission in the Iraqi desert. *Defense Visual Information Center*

Hearts pounding, lungs burning and muscles aching, they finally made it to the alternate site. The team looked it over, and to their disbelief it would not be useable: it was much too small for a CH-46 to get through. The LZ did not look as good as it had on the topographical map; the jungle canopy had closed in, covering most of the area. It was decision time. The Marines knew the longer they stayed in this position, the worse things were going to get. By now the NVA troops in the valley were becoming more active, and it was only a matter of time before they would begin moving up the hill in strength to hunt down the recon team.

The Patrol Leader came up with two alternatives. They could move to find another LZ, which might take them the rest of the day or perhaps two, all the while being pursued by the NVA. The other was to loop back to the primary LZ, which meant going back up the hill where they had engaged the first NVA patrol. The decision was made: Corporal Bierlein took the lesser of two evils, to back up the hill and call for an extract. As they approach the hilltop, RTO Sandoz received word that the "bird was inbound".

When the team reached the LZ they established a defensive perimeter to await extraction. There were still NVA soldiers lying where the initial contact had been made. The team assured that there was no one left alive who could inflict any harm as the team extracted. Corporal Sandoz was now in contact with the incoming Sea Knight helicopter. Not a moment too soon, the aircraft arrived at the LZ and Team Football Star hastened up the rear ramp. The only casualty was Gunnery Sergeant Wilhite, who had picked up some shrapnel. After the team had been extracted, an air strike was called in on the remaining NVA. For his actions on this patrol, Corporal Bierlein would be awarded the Bronze Star with Combat "V."

Such heroic actions were common among these Force Recon teams. Quang Tri, Con Tien, Khe Sahn, Dong Ha; hundreds of names for a thousand acts of courage. For a more in-depth look into the formation and early combat experiences of Marine Force Recon; I highly recommend *Fortune Favors the Brave*, by Bruce F. Meyers; and *Inside Force Recon*, by Michael Lanning and Ray Stubbe. These accounts as well as numerous others will cover more detail than this work permits.

As the Vietnam War was drawing to a close, the Force Recon Companies were deactivated in 1974. As with other special-type forces, the unit was scaled back or absorbed into other units after the war. For example 1st Force would be ensconced into the 1st Reconnaissance Battalion. Here the Recon Marines would provide deep reconnaissance for the 1st Marine Division. Over a decade would pass before the force would be reactivated in 1986. Four years later, 1st Force Reconnaissance Company would be deployed to partake in Operations Desert Shield and Desert Storm during the Gulf War in 1990 and 1991. Here, the Marines would practice their proficiency in deep reconnaissance, in the harsh environment of the Iraqi desert.

The following is an account of such a deep reconnaissance mission, as related by Sergeant Major Hendrik C. "Henk" Brunsveld (ret.):

During the Persian Gulf War, I was with the 24th Marine Expeditionary Unit, in Northern Iraq. I was a Gunnery Sergeant assigned as the Detachment NCOIC of the 2nd Force Recon Detachment, attached to the Command Element of the 24th MEU(SOC).

The Det. had conducted numerous Deep Recon Patrols into Northern Iraq to assess the enemy strength and activities from April 1991 to July 1991. In May 1991 the Iraqis were ordered to withdraw many times by President Bush and then Joint Chiefs of Staff. The Force Recon Marines were tasked with placing eyes on the enemy to accurately report their activities as well as compliance to the U.S. orders. The President had drawn a line along a parallel below which the Iraqi forces were to withdraw. Four other Marines and I were inserted on the evening of 4 May 1991 to observe this withdrawal and report the Iraqi activities.

At a distance of 65 miles, communications were weak and direct support was almost non-existent. So security and clandestine operations were a high priority. The Iraqis had a complete infantry division just 5 to 10 miles north of our position between us and the U.S. forces up north. During the night of the 4th and the 5th everthing was going fine; however, the majority of the Iraqi forces were still in place.

On the morning of the 6th everything changed. During the night, the Iraqis formed their forces into a large column of vehicles and troops, facing south. It appeared they were going to make their final move south as ordered. We reported this activity to higher command. Then around 1000 the convoy moved south; however, at a point still north of our position, they pulled off the main route into the fields. We reported this activity, and waited to observe what it was they were doing. Then about 1200 it became clear, they were redeploying the division along a west to east line. They had moved south, and below the required line in the sand. However, they remained north of our position, which was not good. Around 1400

Weapons and equipment used by a Marine reconnaissance team during Operation Desert Shield include, from left, an M-998 high mobility multi-purpose wheeled vehicle with an M-249 squad automatic weapon (SAW) on top, and an M-998 with an M-2 .50-caliber machine gun. In front of the hard-roofed M-998 is a Marine armed with an M-249 SAW. A Marine armed with an M-16 rifle, equipped with M-209 grenade launcher, is beside the M-998. In front is an M-19 automatic grenade launcher equipped with Starlight scope, center, flanked by an M-60E3, left, and a SAW. Modular universal laser equipment and radio equipment are also shown. *Defense Visual Information Center*

U.S. Marines from the 2nd Force Reconnaissance Company with the 26th MEU(SOC) conduct a Cordon and Search Raid at a suspected Al Qaeda hideout and training site in the Helmand Province of Afghanistan, northwest of Khandahar. These Direct Action raids encompass the other side of Force Recon capabilities, referred to as the "Black Side." *USMC Photo*

because the Marines were watching us too. I signaled my Marines to take cover, and they did accordingly. Then the other Marine with me, at my guidance, stood up and we exposed ourselves to the Iraqi officers. With our weapons up and at the ready, so that they could tell we had M-16s and were in fact American Marines, we walked the long 250 yards back to our position. The whole time we were totally exposed to the five Iraqis on the hill, only 150 yards away.

Once we were back in our position, the Iraqis departed out of sight. For over an hour we communicated with the rear, concerning the new situation. An emergency extract of our team had been ordered, and we were told to be prepared. With the Marine Forces 65 miles away, and all available aircraft already committed, the wait turned into hours.

During the wait, the Iraqis had formed up a Battalion at the base of our hill and were preparing to come up. With this obvious show of threat, the Joint Task Force Commander requested aircraft from the *Aircraft Carrier USS Eisenhower* to launch close air support aircraft, in the form of F-14 Tomcats. Within 20 minutes they arrived and flew at low level over and around our position to warn the Iraqi Forces not to aggress our position. After about 30 minutes of close-in flying the Tomcats became low on fuel and departed for the carrier.

With the threat of the Tomcats gone, and no extract in sight, we once again became very concerned. I sent one of the Sergeants down the slope to observe the Iraqis. After only a few minutes with him in place, suddenly the Sergeant came running. He began yelling, "They're coming, they're coming!" We were not sure if he meant the extract aircraft or the Iraqis. As it turned out it was the Iraqis.

They were coming up the hill in an assault formation, on line with weapons at the assault position. We had only minutes until the firefight, with a superior number of enemy troops.

a small force moved to the base of our hill, which was a ridgeline. After an hour or so, another Marine and I moved down to observe their activity. It appeared the troops were just sitting around, not doing much. Then a small group of what seemed to be officers appeared on a small hill just off the ridgeline we were on. They had spotted the Marines back at our observation position,

With only 5 of us against 250 Iraqis, we were preparing to launch a heavy hail of small arms fire on them to maintain the edge. We had our weapons at the ready, grenades prepared with pins half pulled, and we looked at each other for the last time before the command to fire was given. They were 40 yards away, just below the crest of the hill, and we were full of adrenaline.

Suddenly, a loud thumping sound commenced. Rotor blades appeared directly in front of us, and over the heads of the Iraqi troops to our front. The emergency extract had arrived, with only seconds to spare. With heavy machine guns on board the CH-46 Sea Knight helicopter, the Iraqis stayed down. Once on the ground, we carefully ran back to the aircraft, loaded, and lifted off and away from the near-fight for our lives. The CH-46 flew hard, fast, and low the entire 65 miles back to our position.

Force Recon Marines would continue to be on call, as the United States would deploy its forces in Somalia, Kosovo, and East Timor. After the event of the terrorist attacks on 11 September 2001, the U.S. Marines would again be called upon to mount up and answer the call of a resolute Commander-in-Chief, President George W. Bush, with the battle cry, "Let's Roll!" As of this writing, MEU(SOC) are still deployed in Afghanistan as part of the ongoing Operation Enduring Freedom. Force Recon teams have been involved in a variety of missions, ranging from reconnaissance and enemy interdictions to searching for weapons of mass destruction (WMD). Their mission, true to their Hymn, is to fight where and when their nation calls; they are America's Total Force in Readiness. These are the United States Marines.

Marines' Hymn

From the halls of Montezuma, to the shores of Tripoli,
We fight our country's battles in the air, on land and sea.
First to fight for right and freedom, and to keep our honor clean;
We are proud to claim the title of United States Marines.

Our flag's unfurled to every breeze from dawn to setting sun.
We have fought in every clime and place, where we could take a gun.
In the snow of far off northern lands and in sunny tropic scenes,
You will find us always on the job, The United States Marines.

Here's to health to you and to our Corps which we are proud to serve.
In many a strife we've fought for life and never lost our nerve.
If the Army and the Navy ever look on heaven's scenes,
they will find the streets are guarded by United States Marines.

Marine Air Ground Task Force (MAGTF)

Organization

The Goldwater-Nichols Department of Defense Reorganization Act of 1986 changed the way Force Reconnaissance Companies interfaced into the Marine Corps Warfighting Principles. The act completely overhauled the defense structure of the United States. Operational authority, which previously went through the service chiefs, was now centralized through the Chairman of the Joint Chiefs. The chairman was designated as the principal military advisor to the President, National Security Council, and Secretary of Defense. The act established the position of vice-chairman and streamlined the operational chain of command from the President to the Secretary of Defense to the unified combat commanders.

The Department of Defense (DOD) defines unified combat commands as follows: "Operational Control of the U.S. combat forces is assigned to the nation's Unified Combat Commands. The chain of command runs from the President to the Secretary of Defense to the Unified Commanders in Chief. Orders and other communications from the President or Secretary are transmitted through the Chairman of the Joint Chiefs of Staff. A Unified Combatant Command is composed of forces from two or more services, has a broad and continuing mission and is normally organized on a geographical basis."

The number of Unified Combatant Commands may vary from time to time. Currently there are 10 of them: U.S. European Command, U.S. Pacific Command, U.S. Southern Command, U.S. Central Command, U.S. Joint Forces Command, U.S. Special Operations Command, U.S. Space Command, U.S. Strategic Command, U.S. Transportation Command, and U.S. Northern Command.

With the creation of the U.S. Special Operations Command (SOCOM), this new command became responsible for all special operations forces in the U.S. military. These comprise Army Special Forces, Rangers, and 160th Special Operations Aviation Regiment; Air Force Special Operations Wings and Squadrons; and Navy SEALs.

MAGTF Concept

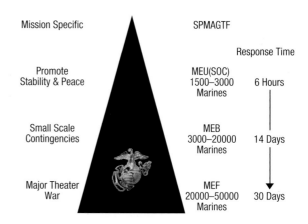

MAGTF

To understand where the Marines fit under this new command, we first need to understand the Marine Air Ground Task Force (MAGTF) structure. The Marines developed the MAGTF as an organization of command, aviation combat, ground combat, and combat service support elements, including Navy Support Elements, and

29

The LHA *USS Tarawa* is an amphibious assault ship which functions as the primary landing ship for assault operations of the MAGTF. The LHA along with the LPD and LSD comprise the Amphibious Ready Group (ARG); these amphibious warships are designed specifically to support an assault from the sea against defended positions ashore. To transport the Marine assault forces ashore, these ships employ the Landing Craft, Air Cushion (LCAC); conventional landing craft; and helicopters. *USMC Photo*

structured it for specific missions. Its combination of components under one command element makes MAGTF a force-multiplier and an effective, powerful organization unlike any other force in the world. General James L. Jones, Commandant of the Marine Corps, relates in the U.S.M.C. document titled *Commandant's Guidance*, "The Marine Air Ground Task Force is both our legacy and the foundation for our future success. Tested and proven in contingencies that span the spectrum from humanitarian assistance to combat, the MAGTF is our (the Marines') operational trademark, having served as our organization framework for employing Marine forces for the last 50 years. MAGTFs join with Amphibious Ready Groups, Carrier Battle Groups, and Maritime Preposition Forces to form a cohesive and cost-effective naval power projection capability." The MAGTF concept is designed to take full advantage of the combat power inherent in air and ground assets by closely integrating them into a single force. The United States maintains the largest and most capable amphibious force in the world. There are four types of MAGTFs: Marine Expeditionary Forces, Marine Expeditionary Brigades, Marine Expeditionary Unit (Special Operations Capable), and Special Purpose MAGTFs.

The Marine Expeditionary Force (MEF) is the largest and most powerful MAGTF, which is a task-organized force designed to fight and win America's battles in conflicts up to and including major-theater war. Commanded by a three-star general, an MEF is composed of one or more full Marine Aircraft Wings, Force Service Support Groups, and complete infantry divisions. An MEF can be adapted to any size dependent upon the mission; an MEF can contain approximately 20,000 to 90,000 Marines, with an average of around 40,000 men and women. There are three MEFs: I MEF based out of Camp Pendleton, California; II MEF, Camp Lejeune, North Carolina; and III MEF in Okinawa, Japan.

Marine Expeditionary Brigades (MEBs) are task-organized to respond to a full range of crises, from forcible entry to humanitarian assistance. The MEB is the Marine Corps' premier response force for the small-scale contingencies that permeate today's global environment. The Marine Corps has three numbered MEBs, one within each MEF with the capability to deploy the MEBs in several ways. Similar to an MEU, an MEB has a 30-day sustainment and deploys 15 amphibious ships, of which five are large-deck ships such as LHA or LHD ships.

The MEU(SOC) is the smaller and most visible type of the Marine-Air Ground Task Force

(MAGTF) Concept, containing an average of 1,500 to 3,000 Marines. It is equipped with all the necessary supplies to sustain itself for up to 30 days of operation and can provide a quick reaction force. There are currently seven MEU(SOC)s in the U.S. Marine Corps. Three are based on the East Coast at Camp Lejeune, North Carolina: the 22nd, 24th, and 26th MEUs. Three are on the West Coast at Camp Pendleton, California: 11th, 13th, and 15th MEUs. One is based in Okinawa, Japan, the 31st MEU. At any given time, two or more of these units are forward deployed. Regardless of the task, the MEU(SOC) stands ready to respond, and can have forces on-site within six hours of getting the "go" call.

Special Purpose MAGTFs (SPMAGTFs) are task-organized to carry out specific missions. The size and capabilities of the SPMAGTF will be dependent on the mission; these operations are normally limited in scope and in focus. Common deployments of a SPMAGTF include raids, noncombatant evacuation, disaster relief, humanitarian assistance, and peacetime engagement activities, or regionally-focused exercises. For example, a SPMAGTF was deployed to Haiti to restore democracy, provide humanitarian assistance, and conduct peacekeeping operations.

MEU(SOC)

Although the Navy placed the SEALs under the new SOCOM command, the Marines were not included. There are a number of theories as to why. The most popular is that the Corps did not want to relinquish command and control of their Marines to a command under control of an Army general. It is also a known fact that during the reorganization, many members of Congress who themselves had served in the Corps, preferred that the Marines maintain their autonomy.

While the Force Recon Marines possessed the same special operations capabilities as their sister services, the consensus was that eventually Force Recon would be absorbed into SOCOM and no longer be a support to the MEUs or MEFs. Consequently, the Marines would not be part of SOCOM and would not be categorized as Special Operations Forces, but rather as Special Operations Capable, or SOC; hence the designator, MEU(SOC). As of this writing, the Corps and SOCOM are revisiting this arrangement.

MEU(SOC) units are specifically groomed for the contingency battles of the future. Based on naval vessels, the forward-deployed MEU(SOC) is uniquely organized, trained, and equipped to provide the naval or Joint force commander with an expeditionary force that is inherently balanced, sustainable, flexible, responsive, and expandable. It is commanded by a colonel, and has a combat strength of approximately 2,000 Marines and Sailors, and is a small yet formidable force-in-

A team of Force Recon Marines having inserted from the sea, they establish a security perimeter as they prepare to cache their LAR-V underwater breathing apparatus gear and move inland to perform a Deep Recon. Once on site, they will remain in the bush for days to provide the MEU(SOC) with vital information and intel.

The Marines of Force Recon are an integral part of the MAGTF, operating as a reconnaissance asset or element of the Maritime Special Purpose Force (MSPF). Here a member of the 4th Force Recon Company provides security for his team as they stop to provide a SitRep.

readiness. Normally deployed aboard three ships of an Amphibious Ready Group (ARG), it is task-organized to accomplish a broad range of mission requirements. The MEU is composed of a command element (CE), a reinforced infantry battalion as the ground combat element (GCE), a reinforced helicopter squadron as the aviation combat element (ACE), and a combat service support element (CSSE), designated the MEU Service Support Group (MSSG).

The MEU(SOC)s are deployed on a six-month cycle to various regions around the world. The MEU(SOC)s are available to the Unified Commanders to handle contingencies arising within their Areas of Responsibility (AOR). The MEU(SOC)s are most frequently deployed within the Pacific, Atlantic, and Indian Oceans, but are available for deployment to any region around the world. With the decline of American bases abroad, the MEU(SOC) is possibly the only U. S. force available to respond rapidly to any world-wide crisis. This availability and readiness has earned the Marines of the MEU(SOC) the mark of distinction as "America's 9-1-1 Force."

The MEU(SOC) is a self-sustained, amphibious combat unit; employing Marine air and ground task force capable of conventional and selected maritime special operation of limited duration in support of a combatant commander. The mission is to provide the geographic combatant commander with a forward-deployed, flexible, sea-based MAGTF capable of rapidly executing Amphibious Operations, designated Maritime Special Operations, Military Operations Other Than War (MOOTW), and Supporting Operations to include enabling the introduction of follow-on-forces. These operations may be conducted at night, under adverse weather conditions, from over the horizon, from sea, by surface, or by air.

MEU(SOC)s provide the regional CINCs a certified, versatile, ready force comprising four major characteristics, as listed in the official USMC policy for Marine Expeditionary Units:

1. Forward presence with operational flexibility. This includes the ability to provide continuous presence and credible, but non-provocative, combat power for rapid employment as the initial response to a crisis. It signals U.S. commitment to the region and is a visible reminder to those who would threaten U.S. interests. It includes engagement activities that shape and promote regional stability.

2. Rapid Response. This is the ability to plan and commence execution of a mission within six hours of receiving an alert, warning, or executive order. It includes the ability to introduce follow-on-MAGTF and joint and/or combined forces by securing staging areas ashore, providing critical command, control, and communication or conducting supporting operations.

3. Task organized for multiple missions. This is the ability to execute a full range of conventional operations, from amphibious assault to humanitarian assistance and disaster relief, as well as selected maritime special operations, across the entire spectrum of conflict, as an integral part of a joint and/or combined campaign, and transition between operational environments on a moment's notice.

4. Sea-based strategic reach with inherent force protection. This is the ability to operate from ships (independent of established airfields, basing agreements, and over-flight rights), providing unimpeded and politically unencumbered access to potential trouble spots around the world. It includes the ability to remain on station, over the horizon of a potential adversary, without revealing exact destinations and/or intentions. Also, it includes the ability to withdraw rapidly at the conclusion of operations.

The core capabilities of a forward-deployed MEU(SOC) are divided into four categories:

1. Amphibious Operations. This is an attack launched from the sea by U.S. Navy and landing forces, embarked in ships or craft involving a landing on a hostile or potentially hostile shore. Amphibious operations include the following phases: planning, embarkation, rehearsal, movement, and assault.

2. Maritime Special Operations. Selected direct action missions are conducted by specially trained, equipped and organized MEU(SOC) forces.

3. Military Operations Other Than War (MOOTW) Operations encompassing the use of military capabilities across the range of military operations short of war. These military actions can be applied to complement any combination of the other instruments of national power and occur before, during, and after war.

4. Supporting Operations. These are operations encompassing the use of military capabilities that support a wide range of potential joint/combined operations.

The following Mission Essential Tasks (METs) provide decision makers, both diplomatic and military, with immediately available and effective crisis responses applicable across the range of MEU(SOC) core capabilities:

Airfield/port seizure: Secure an airfield, port or other key facilities in order to support MAGTF missions, receive follow-on forces, or enable the introduction of follow-on forces (e.g., MPF operations).

Amphibious assault: The principal type of amphibious operation that involves establishing a force on a hostile or potentially hostile shore.

Amphibious demonstration: An amphibious operation conducted for the purpose of deceiving the enemy by a show of force with the expectation of deluding the enemy into a course of action unfavorable to him.

Amphibious raid: An amphibious operation involving swift incursion into or temporary occupation of an objective followed by a planned withdrawal.

Amphibious withdrawal: An amphibious operation involving the extraction of forces by sea in U.S. Navy ships or craft from a hostile or potentially hostile shore.

Anti-terrorism: Defensive measures used to reduce the vulnerability of individuals and property to terrorist acts, to include limited response and containment.

Direct action operations: Short-duration strikes and other small-scale offensive action to seize, destroy, capture, recover, or inflict damage on designated personnel or material. In the conduct of these operations, units may employ raid, ambush, or direct assault tactics; place mines and other munitions; conduct stand-off attacks by fire from air, ground, or maritime platforms; provide terminal guidance for precision-guided munitions; conduct independent sabotage; and conduct anti-ship operations. Such missions may also include counter-proliferation (CP) of Weapons of Mass Destruction (WMD).

Employ non-lethal weapons: Operations planned with intent to minimize fatalities or permanent injuries and limit collateral damage by augmenting forces with non-lethal weapon systems. It should be noted, while political and diplomatic requirements may place the U.S. Marines in such missions (e.g., NEO and peacekeeping) there is simply no such thing as a non-lethal Marine.

Enabling operations: Operations designed to facilitate the smooth transition of follow-on forces into the area of operations. May include chemical/biological assessment, C4 for MAGTF or Joint Task Force higher headquarters and offensive and security operations to seize and secure terrain and/or facilities.

Enhanced urban operations: Encompasses advanced offensive close quarters battle techniques used on urban terrain conducted by units trained to a higher level than conventional infantry. Techniques include advanced breaching, selected target engagement, and dynamic assault techniques using organizational equipment and assets. This is primarily an offensive operation where noncombatants are or may be present and collateral damage must be kept to a minimum.

Fire support planning, coordination, and control in a joint/combined environment: Plan, control, and coordinate fires from naval, air, and ground assets in support of U.S. and/or designated allied/friendly forces.

Humanitarian assistance/disaster relief (HA/DR): Assistance to relieve or reduce the results of natural or man-made disasters or other endemic conditions such as human pain, disease, hunger, or privation that might present a serious threat to life or that can result in great damage to or loss of property. Normally these operations are limited in scope and duration. The assistance provided is designed to supplement or complement the efforts of the host nation, civil authorities, and/or agencies that may have the primary responsibility for providing humanitarian assistance.

Information operations: Actions taken to affect adversary information and information systems while defending one's own information

The Landing Craft, Air Cushioned (LCAC) is a high-speed, over-the-beach, fully amphibious landing craft capable of carrying a 60-75 ton payload, such as an M1A1 MBT. This load-carrying capability, coupled with its speed, allows the LCAC to deliver more Marines on-site and do it in shorter intervals than normal landing craft or AAVs. An M1A1 Main Battle Tank includes a 120mm smoothbore main gun, an NBC overpressure protection system, and an improved armor package. This tank significantly increases the capabilities of the Fleet Marine Forces capable of engaging the enemy out to 4000 meters. *Defense Visual Information Center*

and information systems. A required subtask is Electronic Warfare (EW): any military action involving the use of electromagnetic and directed energy to control the electromagnetic spectrum and/or to attack the enemy.

Intelligence, surveillance, reconnaissance (ISR): Collect, process, integrate, analyze, evaluate, and interpret available information concerning foreign countries, areas, and/or adversaries relative to the mission and area of interest. These include:

Reconnaissance and Surveillance (R&S): A mission undertaken to obtain, by visual observation or other detection methods, information about the activities and resources of an actual or potential enemy, or to secure data concerning the meteorological, hydrographical, or geographical characteristics of a particular area.

Counterintelligence (CI): Information gathered and activities conducted to protect against espionage, adversarial intelligence activities, sabotage, or assassination conducted by or on behalf of foreign powers, organizations, persons, or international terrorist activities, but not including personnel, physical, document or communications security programs.

Signals Intelligence (SIGINT): Intelligence derived from communications, electronics, and foreign instrumentation signals.

Sensor Control and Management Platoon (SCAMP): Performs sensor implant operations, monitors sensors, and reports information generated by sensors.

Limited expeditionary airfield operations: Tactical air operations from austere locations including short-field, unimproved runways.

Non-combatant evacuation operations (NEO): Operations directed by the Department of State whereby noncombatants are evacuated from foreign countries to safe havens or to the U.S., when their lives are endangered by war, civil unrest, or natural disaster.

Peace operations: Encompasses peacekeeping and peace enforcement operations conducted in support of diplomatic efforts to establish and maintain peace.

Provide command, control, communications, and computers (C4): Provide an integrated system of doctrine, procedures, organizational structures, personnel, equipment, facilities, and communications designed to support a commander's exercise of command and control across the range of military operations. Includes providing initial C4 connectivity as the initial entry force of a larger MAGTF, joint and/or combined operation.

Security operations: Protect U.S. (or designated allied/friendly nation) personnel and property. Force Recon Marines may be tasked with providing protection to high-ranking military or civilian members in hostile areas, referred to as Personal Security Detail (PSD). Such a task is usually a high-profile detail in which the Force Recon Marines have the proper maturity, experience, and mindset to keep themselves and a principal safe in the hostile areas of the third world.

Tactical deception operations: Actions executed to deliberately mislead adversary decision makers as to friendly capabilities, intentions, and operations, thereby causing the adversary to take specific actions (or inactions) that will contribute to the accomplishment of the friendly mission. Tactical military deception is planned and conducted to support battles, engagements, and MOOTW.

Tactical recovery of aircraft and personnel (TRAP): Rescue or extract, by surface or air, downed aircraft and/or personnel and equipment; provide aircraft sanitization; and provide advanced trauma-life support in a benign or hostile environment.

Terminal guidance operations (TGO): The guidance applied to a guided missile between midcourse guidance and arrival in the vicinity of the target. Electronic, mechanical, visual, or other assistance given to aircraft, missiles, ships, and artillery assets to facilitate arrival at, operation within or over, landing upon, or departure from an air/beach landing or airdrop facility.

Visit, board, search and seizure (VBSS) operations: The conduct of vessel boarding/seizure in support of Maritime Interception Operations (MIO) on a cooperative or uncooperative vessel, whether it is pier-side, at anchor, or underway.

One mission has recently been removed from Force Recon's task list, this being In-Extremis Hostage Rescue, or IHR. Such missions fall under USSOCOM (United States Special Operations Command) Tier 1 units (i.e., Combat Applications Group (CAG), Delta Force, and DevGrp (formerly SEAL Team Six)) which have primary responsibility of any hostage recovery. It was recognized IHR teams demanded extensive training to achieve and maintain an intense level of proficiency. Consequently, the IHR mission was relinquished totally to SOCOM assets and taken off the Marines' menu. While the Marines are no longer tasked with IHR, it should be noted other missions, such as Maritime Interdiction Operations, VBSS (Visit, Board, Search and Seizure), GOPLAT (Gas/Oil Platforms), prisoner recovery, and the like, still require the Force Recon Marines to be just as proficient in Close Quarters Battle (CQB) skills and surgical shooting techniques. As always, the Corps still maintains the highest standard of precision shooting and is capable of IHR should the need arise.

Command Element

The Command Element (CE) provides the command, control, communications, computers, and intelligence (C4I) required for effective planning and execution of operations. The CE is composed of:

Force Reconnaissance Company (FORECON) detachment: Provides direct action capability and ground reconnaissance within the MEU(SOC) commander's area of interest.

Radio Battalion (RadBn) detachment: Provides an

Light Armored Vehicle-25 (LAV-25) provides the MAGTF with strategic mobility to reach and engage any threat. The tactical mobility and effective use of firepower to defeat soft and armored targets. Marines from Alpha Company, 2nd Light Armored Vehicle Company, attached to the Battalion Landing Team 3/6 26th Marine Expeditionary Unit (Special Operations Capable), prepare their LAV-25 to conduct a patrol around Khandahar International Airport during Operation Enduring Freedom. One Marine is at the ready, manning the 7.62mm machine gun atop the M242 25mm chain gun in the turret. In the background is the Khandahar control tower with "Texas 17," the Marine call sign for the area. Other variants of the LAV are Light Armored Vehicle-Command and Control (LAV-C2), Light Armored Vehicle-Anti-Tank (LAV-AT), Light Armored Vehicle-Logistics (LAV-L), Light Armored Vehicle-Mortar (LAV-M), Light Armored Vehicle-Recovery (LAV-R). *USMC Photo*

enhanced capability for SIGINT collection, analysis, and electronic warfare (EW). A radio reconnaissance team (RRT) capability is included for advance force employment during selected operations.

Communications Battalion (CommBn): Responsible for command and control communications for all operations.

Mobile Command and Control Team (MCCT): Provides Joint Task Force, SOF, or follow-on-force enabling capability.

Additionally there is an Intelligence Battalion Detachment that provides intelligence support for all operations. It includes:

Human Intelligence Exploitation Team (HET): Provides counterintelligence and interrogation/document translation support.

Force Imagery Interpretation Unit (FIIU): Provides limited imagery interpretation support.

The AAV7 is an armored assault amphibious full-tracked landing vehicle. The vehicle carries troops in water operations from ship to shore, through rough water and surf zone. It also carries troops to inland objectives after ashore. It carries a crew of three and 21 combat-equipped troops. Cruising range on land at 25 miles per hour is 300 miles; it can cruise on water for 7 hours at 2,600 rpm. Cruising speed on land is 20-30 miles per hour, and on water 6 miles per hour. Armament is one M-2 .50-cal. machine gun and one MK 19 MOD3 40mm machine gun. *Defense Visual Information Center*

Topographic (TOPO) Platoon: providing limited cartography and terrain model building capability.

Sensor Control and Management Platoon (SCAMP): Plans the employment of, operates, maintains, and reports information generated from remote sensor systems.

Marine Liaison Element Detachment, providing fire control capabilities for Joint, Combined, and coalition forces working in concert with the MEU.

Ground Combat Element (GCE)

The Ground Combat Element (GCE) Battalion Landing Team (BLT) is a reinforced infantry battalion of approximately 1,200 Marines. The GCE would include:

Commanding Officer

Executive Officer and staff

Headquarters and Service (H&S) Company

Scout Sniper Platoon

Three Infantry Companies

Weapons Company

Artillery Battery with six 155mm howitzers

Light Armored Reconnaissance (LAR) detachment, configured with 7 to 16 Light Armored Vehicles (LAV): Provides mobile reconnaissance, screening and strike capability with its LAVs and organic scouts.

Assault Amphibian Vehicle (AAV) platoon, configured with 15 AAVs: Provides amphibious-assault, ship-to-shore movement and ground mobility.

Combat Engineer platoon: Provides mobility enhancement, survivability, counter-mobility, and general engineer support.

Reconnaissance platoon: Provides ground reconnaissance and surveillance, and intelligence collection and reporting within the MEU(SOC) commander's area of influence.

Shore Fire Control Party (SFCP): Provides naval

surface fire support; and tank platoon; configured with four M1A1 main battle tanks. Provides a limited heavy armor capability to ground forces ashore.

Air Combat Element (ACE)

The Air Combat Element (ACE) is a reinforced helicopter squadron including fixed-wing fighter/attack aircraft units flying the AV-8B Harrier attack aircraft and the F/A-18 Hornet. In addition to the fighters, two KC-130 aircraft based in continental United States (CONUS) are available for deployment. The ACE is mission-organized to afford assault support, fixed-wing and rotary-wing close air support, airborne command and control, and low-level, close-in air defense. The ACE is structured as follows:

Commanding Officer
Executive Officer and staff
Marine Medium Helicopter Squadron (HMM) detachment: Provides medium-lift assault support, configured with twelve CH-46E helicopters (plans are for the CH-46 to be replaced by the MV-22).
Marine Heavy Helicopter Squadron (HMH) detachment, configured with four CH-53E helicopters: Provides extended-range, heavy-lift assault support.
Marine Light Attack Squadron (HMLA) detachment: Configured with four AH-1W attack helicopters and two or three UH-1N utility helicopters: Provides close air support, airborne command and control, and escort.
Marine Attack Squadron (VMA) or Fighter/Attack Squadron (VMFA) detachment, configured with six AV-8B Harrier or F/A-18 aircraft: Provides organic close air support.
Marine Aerial Refueler/Transport Squadron (VMGR) detachment, configured with two KC-130 aircraft: Provides refueling services for embarked helicopters and aircraft, and

The CH-46E Sea Knight helicopter first entered service with the Marines in 1964 to meet the medium-lift requirements in Vietnam. The mission of the CH-46E Sea Knight helicopter is to provide all-weather, day/night, night vision goggle (NVG) assault transport of combat troops, supplies, and equipment during amphibious and subsequent operations ashore. This Sea Knight is loaded with a Combat Rubber Raiding Craft (CRRC) as it lifts off, preparing for a "Soft Duck" insertion. Range is 132 nautical miles (151.8 miles) for an assault mission; speed is 145 knots. The normal crew of four includes pilot, copilot, crew chief, and 1st mechanic; in combat, the crew of five is the pilot, copilot, crew chief, and two aerial gunners; combat payload is a maximum of 14 troops with aerial gunners; for medical evacuation it is 15 litter patients and 2 attendants.

performs as required other support tasks, including parachute operations, flare drops, and cargo transportation. Maximum flexibility is maintained with an airborne command, control and coordination capability. The detachment trains with the MEU throughout the Pre-deployment Training Program (PTP), and then is on CONUS standby, prepared to deploy within 96 hours.

The CH/RH-53D Sea Stallion helicopter is the Marine Corps' medium lift helicopter. It is designed for the transportation of equipment, supplies, and personnel during the assault phase of an amphibious operation and subsequent operations ashore. CH-53E Super Stallion helicopter is the Corps' heavy-lift helicopter designed for the transportation of material and supplies. The 53E is equipped with a refueling probe, giving the helicopter indefinite range. The helicopter seats 37 passengers and centerline seating can carry 55 passengers. Here, a Sea Stallion with the 26th MEU(SOC) takes on fuel at a forward aerial refueling site operated by the Marine Wing Support Squadron 273 at the Khandahar International Airport in Khandahar, Afghanistan. *USMC Photo*

Maritime Special Purpose Force (MSPF)

The MSPF is task-organized from MEU(SOC) assets to provide a special-operations-capable force that can be quickly tailored to accomplish a specific mission, and employed either as a complement to conventional MAGTF operations or in the execution of a selected maritime special operations mission. Particular emphasis is placed on operations requiring precision skills that normally are not resident in traditional amphibious raid companies. Command and control of the MSPF will remain with the MEU(SOC) commander. The MSPF is not designed to duplicate exist-

ing capabilities of SOF, but is intended to focus on operations in a maritime environment. The MSPF is not capable of operating independently of its parent MEU; however, it is capable of conducting operations with, or in support of, SOF. The MSPF task organization can be enhanced with the addition of the ARG's Naval Special Warfare Task Unit (NSWTU) detachment.

The common structure of the MSPF follows, (this may vary upon mission dependent requirements): Command Element, Assault Element, R/S Platoon and Security Element.

Command Element (CE): Commander of the MSPF will be designated by the MEU(SOC) commander. The command element is normally structured as follows: the MSPF is divided into HQs (MSPF Commander, Forward Air Controller (always a pilot), radio operators, and marshalling area control officer (usually an Gunnery Sergeant or Master Sergeant from the Force Recon Detachment), Human Exploitation Team (HET), and Medical support.

Assault Element (AE): The AE is the main component of the MSPF. These are the shooters, and they are organized to perform assault, explosive breaching, internal security, and sniper functions. The assault function normally will be executed by the FORECON detachment. Mission-specific augmentation (e.g., additional sniper support, specialized demolitions, explosive ordnance disposal, SIGINT/EW, etc.) will be provided from other MEU(SOC) assets or from the NSWTU embarked with the ARG. Concerning the sniper function, Captain Christian explains, "While each Force Recon platoon does have sniper capability, when deployed with the MSPF that responsibility falls into the Battalion Recon Marine mission; as every

(Force Recon) man will be needed to kick doors and shoot."

R/S Platoon: The Recon and Surveillance team is the sniper support for the Assault Element. Usually made up from the Recon Battalion platoon and augmented from the BLT sniper platoon, they have an RRT (Radio Recon Team) attached. The RRT team will listen in on and jam the enemy's radio frequency. Usually they have special language skills to listen in on enemy radio traffic.

Security Element: The security element will isolate the target building and provide additional "Trailer" support to the Force Recon detachment. They are essentially a rifle platoon with special skills and training. These individuals will follow Force Recon Marines into the target, and cover danger areas so a shooter can continue his mission of clearing the house, hence the term "trailers." The security element is normally composed of selected members from the BLT and may be augmented by the NSWTU (e.g., SEALs) embarked with the ARG. The security element will act as a reinforcing unit, a support unit, a diversionary unit, or an extraction unit. The trailers will assist with dead and wounded shooters and the collection of intel.

Marine Service Support Group (MSSG): Otherwise known as "Beans, Bullets and Band Aids," this group provides a full range of combat service support necessary to accomplish all assigned missions. It is organized to provide supply, maintenance, transportation, deliberate engineering, medical and dental care, automated information processing, utilities, landing support (port/airfield support operations), disbursing, and legal and postal services to the entire MEU(SOC). The support

The AH-1W Super Cobra helicopter provides fire support and security for forward and rear-area forces. This includes point target/anti-armor and anti-helicopter duty, armed escort, supporting arms control and coordination, point and limited-area air defense from enemy fixed-wing aircraft, and armed and visual reconnaissance. The Cobra is armed with a 20mm turreted cannon, four external wing points that can fire 2.75-inch/5.0-inch rockets, and an assortment of precision-guided missiles, including TOW/Hellfire (point target/anti-armor), Sidewinder (anti-air), and Sidearm (anti-radar). *Defense Visual Information Center*

element normally is composed of assets from the BLT Reconnaissance Platoon and Scout Sniper Platoon (R&S/sniper support) coupled with elements of the ACE, Radio Bn Det, COMM Det, and HET assets from the MEU(SOC) CE. Additional capability may be provided by the NSWTU embarked with the ARG. The support element is normally structured as follows:

a) Team(s), Reconnaissance and Scout Sniper Platoons.

b) Team(s), Communications Detachment.

c) Team(s), Radio Battalion Detachment.

d) Team(s), HET Det.

e) NSWTU, PHIBRON (as required).

f) Aviation Support Element: Capable of precise night-vision flying and navigation, various insertion/extraction means and Forward Arming and Refueling Point (FARP) operations. The specific structure of the aviation support element will vary depending on the lift requirements and distance to the crisis site.

The UH-1N is a twin-piloted, twin-engine helicopter. It is used in support operations such as command and control with a specialized communication package (ASC-26), supporting arms coordination, and assault support. The UH-1N also can provide medical evacuation for up to six litter patients and one medical attendant. It can carry external cargo and perform search and rescue using a rescue hoist. Further, it can undertake reconnaissance and reconnaissance support, and special operations using a new navigational thermal imaging system mission kit. Its range is 172 nautical miles (197.8 miles). Crew consists of one officer and two enlisted men. Armament mounted on each side of the aircraft can be a M-240 7.62mm machine gun or the GAU-16 .50-caliber machine gun or the GAU-17 7.62mm automatic gun. All three weapons systems are crew-served, and the pilot can also control the GAU-2B/A in the fixed forward firing mode. The helicopter can also carry two 7-shot or 19-shot 2.75-inch rocket pods. *Defense Visual Information Center*

Subordinate Element Tasks

The MEU(SOC) is task-organized and trained to operate with Special Operations Forces (SOF) as mission requirements dictate. This interoperability may be in the role of a supporting force or as the supported force if directed by Joint Task Force Commander employing the force. The Naval Special Warfare Training Unit (NSWTU) (SEALS/Special Boat Unit (SBU) embarked aboard amphibious shipping may be employed in a supporting/supported role with the Maritime Special Purpose Force (MSPF) or other elements of the MEU(SOC). Effective operational and tactical interoperability between the MEU(SOC) and the embarked NSWTU, across the spectrum of MEU(SOC) operations, is essential. Prior to deployment, the MEU(SOC) will be required to demonstrate interoperability with the NSWTU.

The Carrier Battle Group (CVBG) may operate in support of an MEU(SOC) conducting operations from the sea, or an MEU(SOC) may be in support of a maritime operation. Effective interoperability is achieved through a series of combined leadership training events such as the Joint Maritime Tactics Course, combined at-sea training, and a formal evaluation. These training events, when practical, can be used to provide insight into the interoperability of the Amphibious Ready Group (ARG)/MEU and CVBG.

MEU(SOC) Pre-deployment Training Program (PTP)

The MEU(SOC) commander is responsible for the Pre-deployment Training Program (PTP) of his command. Progressive improvement in individual and unit skills allows an MEU to execute a full range of conventional and selected maritime special operations missions. This is accomplished by means of a dedicated and intensive PTP of about 26 weeks. The PTP is designed to integrate the Amphibious Squadron (PHIBRON) and MEU, as well as other designated U.S. Navy forces (e.g., NSWTU and CVBGs), to optimize their inherent capabilities. The MEU commander requires external training assistance from Force Commanders and agencies outside of the U.S. Marine Corps, because of the nature of the specialized training and the sensitivity of the maritime special operations mission. Close coordination with respective U.S. Navy commands will ensure that appropriate interoperability training among U.S. Navy and Marine Corps units is accomplished throughout the initial collective, intermediate, and final training phases of the PTP cycle.

MEU(SOC) Certification Policy

The certification process is continuous in nature and encompasses training events and evaluations throughout the entire PTP. Only those MEUs that have been certified can be designated as SOC. MEU(SOC)s are capable of executing the full range of core capabilities\ and mission-essential tasks (MET) as described above. The SOC evaluation and certification process includes tests to evaluate conventional and selected maritime special operations capabilities, and requires the MEU to plan and conduct multiple missions simultaneously. Known as a SOCEX, Special Operations Capable Exercise, this qualification exercise evaluates the MEU capability of performing each of its missions. This SOC certifica-

The mission of the AV-8B Harrier II is to attack and destroy surface and air targets, to escort helicopters, and to conduct other such air operations as may be directed. It is armed with seven external store stations, comprising six wing stations for AIM-9 Sidewinder and an assortment of air-to-ground weapons, external fuel tanks, and AGM-65 Maverick missiles; and one centerline station for DECM pod or air-to-ground ordnance or a GAU-12 25mm six-barrel gun pod. *Defense Visual Information Center*

tion encompasses the ARG as well as the MEU. Just as in their missions, there is no margin for error. If a failure occurs in the training process, the force must remediate, and qualify prior to deployment.

Utilizing the MAGTF concept, the U.S. Marine Corps stands poised and prepared to engage a ready reaction force on-site to achieve National Command Authority goals. Whether the mission calls for a specialized unit such as the SPMAGTF, or a larger presence with the deployment of the MEF; the MAGTF concept provides the versatility of expanding the amount of forces while still maintaining the continuity of the task force. With MEU(SOC) constantly on deployments around the globe, the Marines are ready to defend freedom and uphold democracy, anywhere and anytime.

Force Recon

Now that we have examined the MAGTF concept, let's focus on where Force Reconnaissance (FORECON) fits into this warfighting model. There is one organic Force Reconnaissance Company ADCON/OPCON (Administrative Command/Operational Control) to each MEF: 1st Force Recon Company is assigned to I MEF, MARFORPAC, Camp Pendleton, California; 2nd Force Recon Company is with II MEF, MARFORLANT, Camp Lejeune, North Carolina; and 3rd Recon is with 3rd MarDiv, III MEF, Camp S.D. Butler, Okinawa, Japan (where a Force Recon detachment who works for the MEF commander is attached rather than a whole company). Additionally, there exist two Reserve units, 3rd and 4th Force Reconnaissance, which fall under Marine Forces Reserve (MarForRes); 3rd Force is in Mobile, Alabama and 4th Force is in Hawaii with a Det in Reno, NV.

Force Recon and Battalion Recon

Worth noting is that within the MAGTF there are two reconnaissance units; one of these is Force Reconnaissance Company, while the other is the Battalion Recon (though sometimes referred to as Division Recon) Platoon, which is under the commander of the Combat Element. The Force Recon Company works directly for the MEF Commanding General, normally a three-star, or directly for the MEU(SOC) commander, providing tactical and strategic reconnaissance and limited scale raids such as GOPLAT, VBSS, and demolition raids, in the deep battle space. Force Recon covers the commander's area of *interest*: the edge of the artillery fan and beyond. The Battalion Recon covers the commander's area of *influence*: within the

artillery fan, approximately 30 kilometers from the forward line of troops. The Force Reconnaissance Company will conduct operational-level reconnaissance in the deep battle areas. Conversely, Battalion Recon Marines are trained to operate just forward of the frontlines or directly in front of or alongside of the conventional Marine units.

Not all Battalion Recon Marines are Airborne and/or SCUBA qualified. While the training paths are similar for the Recon Marines, those assigned to Force Reconnaissance Companies will receive more advanced skills and training, which will more than match those of the Special Operations Forces of SOCOM. This skill set will allow the Force Recon Marines to excel in the area of Deep Reconnaissance and Direct Action (DA) missions, well beyond the range of the Battalion Recon assets.

Types of Reconnaissance

According to Marine Corps doctrine there are four basic types of reconnaissance: Route, Area, Zone and Force-Orientated. Each of these in turn provides specific intelligence for mission planning and situational awareness. These types of recon are defined as follows: *Route Reconnaissance* is intended to acquire detailed information of a specific route and all terrain from which the enemy could influence movement along that route. This type of recon focuses along a specific line of communication, such as a road, railway, or waterway. Route recon usually precedes the movement of friendly forces. *Area Reconnaissance* is designed to gather information on terrain or enemy activity with a prescribed area, such as a town, ridgeline, woods, bridge, building, or installation. Emphasis

The Marine Hymn reads, "We have fought in every clime and place." This is evident in this view showing the assortment of uniforms and equipment to accomplish any mission given. Rear row (l-r): new issue USMC "Pixel" camouflage, Desert, Arctic and HALO; front row, (l-r) CQB, Sniper, and Combatant Diver. All dressed up and good to go!

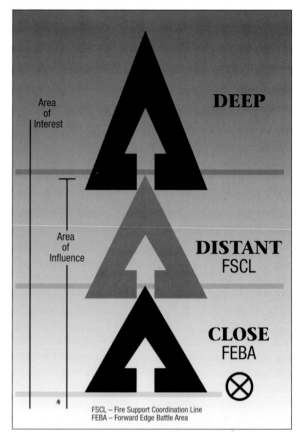

Area of Interest

Area of Influence

DEEP

DISTANT FSCL

CLOSE FEBA

⊗

FSCL – Fire Support Coordination Line
FEBA – Forward Edge Battle Area

is placed on reaching the area without being detected. *Zone Reconnaissance* is conducted to obtain information on all routes, obstacles, terrain and enemy forces within a zone defined by boundaries. This type of recon concerns itself with the total integrated intelligence picture of the battle area defined by length and breadth. The size of the zone depends on the potential for information on enemy forces, terrain, and weather in the zone. The parameters for zone recon are determined by the commander and the recon forces available to exploit the intelligence value of the zone. *Force-Orientated Reconnaissance* is focused not on a geographic area but on a specific enemy organization, regardless of where it is located or where it may move. Force-Orientated recon deals with

Reconnaissance missions are characterized by the depth of penetration they require having impact in terms of time, risk coordination, and support requirements. **Close Recon** is conducted in the area extending forward of the FEBA to the FSCL. Combat units manning the FEBA usually conduct close recon. **Distant Recon** is concerned with the location, disposition, composition and movement of enemy forces. Distant recon is conducted beyond the FSCL to the limits of the commander's area of influence. Finally, **Deep Recon**, which is conducted beyond the commander's area of influence to the limits of the commander's area of interest. Such recon is usually directed toward ascertaining the disposition of enemy reinforcements.

intelligence information required about a specific enemy or target unit. The recon team will shadow the enemy unit, moving when it moves and observing and reporting all pertinent information.

Force Reconnaissance Missions

Force Reconnaissance (FORECON) is employed as an asset to the MEU(SOC); it is in direct support of the MEU's operational directives and thereby a direct support of the MEF Commander. The FORE-CON mission is to conduct amphibious reconnaissance, surveillance, and direct action missions. The DOD dictionary defines reconnaissance as, "A mission undertaken to obtain, by visual observation or other detection methods, information about the activities and resources of an enemy or potential enemy, or to secure data concerning the meteorological, hydrographic, or geographic characteristics of a particular area. Also called RECON." Surveillance is defined as, "The systematic observation of aerospace, surface or subsurface areas, places, person, or thing by visual, aural, electronic photographic or other means." Further differentiation is made as follows, "Surveillance complements reconnaissance by cueing the commitment of reconnaissance assets against specific locations or specially targeted enemy units. Surveillance provides information while reconnaissance answers the commander's specific questions." The Force Reconnaissance Marines are the eyes and ears of the MEF Commander. They are the boots on the ground and the eyes on the target, providing him with immediate intel in the "Deep Battle" area.

Mission or tasks are characterized by Force Reconnaissance as either "Green Side" or "Black Side" operations. "Green Side" operations included in these mission profiles are tasks including: the conduct of deep preassault and postassault reconnaissance. These operations would serve to observe, identify, and report enemy activity and collect information of military importance to the MEU. Postassault reconnaissance could include such tasks as bomb damage assessment or BDA. Force Recon Marines may also be employed to gather terrain reconnaissance—tasks which include hydrographic recon of beaches, and intel on bridges, roadways, urban areas, helicopter landing zones, airborne drop zones, landing zones for Landing Craft Air Cushion (LCAC), and forward operating sites for aircraft operations.

Members of 1st Platoon, 4th Force Reconnaissance Company rise from the water and approach the beach wearing LAR-V rebreathers. Whether inserting from the sea, or from the air via helicopter or parachute, the Marines of Force Recon are highly trained in infiltration techniques and use whatever means necessary to execute their mission.

Stealth and concealment are among the hallmarks of the Force Recon Marines. Here a team "takes a knee" during a security stop as they make their way deep into enemy lines. The team automatically assumes a "tight 360-inch posture, ensuring every sector around the team is being covered. All of these actions are done in a deliberate and fluid motion, and in complete silence.

Following in the footsteps of their "pathfinder" predecessors, they can conduct initial terminal guidance (ITG) for helicopters, landing craft, and airborne troops. FORECON teams may also collect tactical imagery, both film and digital, as well as place and recover ground remote sensors and beacons. They may also be utilized as a counter-reconnaissance asset.

While the primary mission of Force Reconnaissance is indeed that of reconnaissance and surveillance, there are times when their mission requires them to be more proactive. These are Direct Action (DA) missions or "Black Side" and would include, but not be limited to, direction of terminal guidance of precision-guided munitions

or smart bombs. A prime example of this was seen during the Gulf War and in Operation Enduring Freedom in Afghanistan, in the calling in of close air support (CAS) and the adjusting for direct and indirect fire support assets. Direct Action missions would also include Maritime Interdiction Operations (MIO) such as raids on Gas/Oil Platforms (GOPLATS). An example of this was Operation Praying Mantis in the Persian Gulf. Here, on 18 April 1988, members of 4th Platoon, 2nd Force Recon Company were instrumental in assaulting and neutralizing the Sassan oil/gas platform, where Iranian troops posed a threat to U.S. forces. Other DA missions include Visit/Board/Search/Seizure (VBSS) as well as the capture and recovery of selected enemy personnel and equipment. Force Recon Marines are also schooled in sniper and demolition skills and can be employed as set forth by their mission parameters.

Force Recon Marines are involved in a vast array of missions. As Gunnery Sergeant Tim Hatcher, 5th Platoon, 2nd Force Recon Company relates, "[we] Participated in Operation Desert Storm (with 7th Platoon, 1st Force Recon Company). . . . Conducted clandestine reconnaissance and surveillance on Iraqi positions inside the Kuwaiti border to include the Al Wahfra Forest. . . . My team had the opportunity to test our Close Air Support skills upon the Iraqis the day prior to their slipping into Kahfji. . . . While there, we conducted observation from static positions and spider holes.

"Participated in Operation Restore Hope (with 7th Platoon, 1st Force Recon Company). . . . My team as well as then Sergeant Kevin Daly's (now a Gunnery Sergeant) swam for two hours into port facility to the north of Mogadishu airport. . . . We were eyes-on and in-place fire support for the incoming Raid Company. . . . While there, we conducted Personal Security Details (PSD) for General Johnston and Colonel Wilhelm. . . . We also conducted observation from static positions. . . . Our platoon also conducted a Direct Action raid on an

Reconnaissance and surveillance is the "Green Side" of Force Recon missions. Here, a Recon Marine is using a pair of M19 binoculars. This binocular has 7-power magnification with a 50mm-objective lens. One side of the binoculars has a laminated reticle pattern that consists of a vertical and horizontal mil scale that is graduated in 10-mil increments. Using this reticle pattern aids the observer in determining range and adjusting indirect fires. In addition to that application, the binoculars are used in observing target areas and enemy movement and positions, identifying aircraft, improving low-light-level viewing, and estimating range.

arms market and a long-range reconnaissance mission further into Somalia."

All in a day's work for the Force Recon Marine!

Table of Organization

The Table of Organization (T/O) for Force Recon has varied over the years. While 1st Force Recon Company operated separate from the 1st Recon Battalion, 2nd Force was organic to 2nd Recon Battalion. However, in July 2002 the USMC reorganized

Making the grade as a member of the U.S. Marines is a challenging task to say the least; making the further commitment to belong to a Force Recon Company is even more demanding. What kind of person joins Force Recon? These men are definitely Type A personalities;

A quick drive through the company parking lot with its collection of off-road vehicles, mountain and touring bikes, kayaks, skydiving and scuba gear, etc., will give you an insight into these "high speed warriors." It's a way of life that says, "If you're not living on the edge, you are taking up too much room!"

Taking this a step farther, Captain Andy Christian of 2nd Force Reconnaissance Company formed the Force Recon Extreme Team. Captain Christian, who is a "mustang" (a formerly enlisted Marine), has competed in over 20 triathlons and exemplifies the quintessential leader in the Force Recon community. The intent of the team was to compete in adventure races and serve as a recruiting tool to display what the Corps was about and attract potential recruits to the Marines in general, and Recon in particular. The Mission Statement of the Force Recon Extreme Team reads, "The mission of the 2nd Force Reconnaissance Company Extreme Racing Team is to recruit qualified applicants for duty within the Reconnaissance Community. We will accomplish this by demonstrating the professionalism, esprit de corps and physical endurance embodied in all Reconnaissance Marines. The final result desired is to attract civilians and Marines for potential selection and training with the United States Marine Corps Force/Battalion Reconnaissance Units." For more information on the Force Recon Extreme Team visit: www.forcereconextreme.com.

the Force Recon Companies to bring them more in line with the traditional organizational structure, and currently both 1st and 2nd Force Reconnaissance units are now stand-alone companies.

Although Force Recon is a company, it conducts operations as a battalion. A Force Recon Company is composed of a Company Headquarters Section, with a Lieutenant Colonel Commanding Officer (CO), an Executive Officer (XO), a Major, and a Sergeant Major. Supporting the operational platoons is the S1 (Administrative), the S2 (Intelligence), the S3 (Operations, under which is the Training Cell and Paraloft), the S4 (Logistics and Supply, which oversees the Dive and Amphibious Lockers, the Motor Transport Section, and the Armory), and the S6 (Communications) Section. There are approximately 200 Marines and Sailors in the Company.

Each company will have six operational platoons. The Operational platoons are staffed with

No, this is *not* a Navy SEAL! Force Recon Marines are trained Combatant Divers and receive the same training as their naval comrades in the science of open- and closed-circuit underwater breathing systems. Also worth noting is that this Marine is swimming in with a fully loaded rucksack, destined for a deep recon mission behind enemy lines.

Seen here, a sniper with a 7.62mm M40A1 and his spotter have gotten into position and lie in wait for their prey. They could be in position for hours or days. For a sniper team, patience is not only a virtue; it is a matter of survival.

a platoon headquarters consisting of a Platoon Commander (Captain), a platoon sergeant (a Staff Sergeant or Gunnery Sergeant), Platoon Radio Operator (normally a Staff Sergeant or Gunnery Sergeant), a Navy Special Amphibious Reconnaissance Corpsman (SARC), and a platoon Equipment NCO (Rigger/Armorer). Worth noting is that there are significantly more senior NCOs than in conventional forces. Force Recon companies look for Marines with maturity and a higher level of responsibility; consequently, this usually equates to a more senior rank and time in service. Additionally, the amount of time it takes to go through the training cycle adds to this ratio.

Each operational platoon is composed of three six-man teams, which is a departure from

The Force Recon Marines are resourceful and highly motivated. The nastier the environment the better: cold and wet or hot and swampy. They will cross whatever terrain necessary to infiltrate and prosecute their mission. They will be where you least expect them; then again, where you expect them they will not be. Here, members of 6th Platoon, 2nd Force Recon Company wade across a stream performing an infiltration.

Whether calling in a SitRep or Close Air Support, keeping in close contact with the MEU(SOC) provides the commander with real-time intelligence to launch an assault against enemy forces. Here SSgt Joe Tablada of 1st Platoon, 4th Force Recon calls in a SitRep safely concealed in the jungle vegetation.

the traditional four-man team concept. The six-man team T/O represents a functionality based on real world needs, that is, new surveillance and communications equipment. The new Digital comm gear coming on-line (cameras, computers, and so forth) is lighter, stronger and more efficient than previous gear, but there is more of it. Because of the additional equipment, a four-man team could not transport all the necessary equipment required for Deep Reconnaissance missions. Taking into account the Recon team will have to insert by jumping, diving, or walking, carrying the required equipment to complete the mission, the additional manpower is essential to the success of

the mission. Another factor favoring the transformation is the fact that when conducting Deep Reconnaissance, stealth and vigilance is the basis for survival. A six-man team possesses a suitable number of team members to provide an adequate rest period while preserving security. Additionally important is what actions the team has to take should it incur a casualty. The six-man team can double up gear if necessary, whereas a four-man team might have to cache some of its equipment in order to evacuate a wounded teammate.

The typical organization of a Force Recon team consists of: a Recon Team Leader (TL), an Assistant Team Leader (ATL), Field Radio Operator, Recon

Referred to as a Maritime Interdiction Operation or MIO, Force Recon Marines fast-rope from a Huey helicopter onto the bow area of the ship. Once the team has been inserted, it will immediately secure the wheelhouse, taking control of the ship. *Courtesy 2nd Force Recon. USMC*

Man, Recon/Scout, and Recon Scout/Driver. Captain Andy Christian, Platoon Commander, 6th Platoon, 2nd Force Recon Company, describes the Roles and Responsibility of the team members for the six-man team is as follows:

"The point man is responsible for early detection of enemy, and is usually a sergeant. He assists the primary land navigator with all phases of the patrol. Depending on team assignments he also has a collateral job as POW search team and demo team.

"The navigator is a sergeant whose primary responsibility is navigation. He selects the route, briefs TL, and together they decide on what the primary and alternate route will be. He has several collateral duties to include POW search team and demo team. On the objective, the point man and navigator can make up an R/S team.

"The primary communicator, a sergeant, is a school-trained communications expert. He will carry the PRC-117 TACSAT. He is responsible for all the team's communications gear. He will determine communication requirements and execute the communication plan. He will ensure the Digital Communication, TACSAT, VHF, HF, UHF radio procedures are in place.

"The assistant communicator, a sergeant, is a reconnaissance Marine cross trained to operate as an assistant radio operator. He has the same mission as the primary RTO. He usually carries the HF radio while on patrol. He will be familiar with all phases of the communication plan. He will take over as the Primary RTO in the event of death or injury.

"The assistant team leader, a sergeant or staff sergeant, is second in command. He is responsible for enforcing all SOPs for the team. He is the team leader's right-hand man. He will ensure all the warning order tasks are being adhered to so the team leader can focus on the mission. (These enforcements take place before the patrol begins.) However, he is responsible for bringing up the rear of the patrol. He makes sure the team head

During Operation Praying Mantis in the Persian Gulf in April 1988, members of the 4th Platoon, 2nd Force Recon Company inspect a ZU-23 23mm automatic anti-aircraft gun on the Iranian Sassan oil/gas platform. A combined team of Force Recon Marines and SEALS performed a GOPLAT or Gas/Oil Platform, direct action mission. This mission was carried out after the *USS Samuel B. Roberts* (FFG-58), a guided missile frigate, struck an Iranian mine. *Defense Visual Information Center*

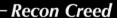
count is up, and that the team is adhering to the Platoon SOP. He is the team enforcer!

"The team leader, a staff sergeant, is responsible for whatever the team does or fails to do. He is the Marine who makes all the key decisions concerning insertion, mission, extraction, etc."

What about officers in Force Recon: Do they go out with the teams on a Recon patrol? Captain Christian commented on this, "As an Officer would I lead a patrol? Unlikely! The Platoon Commander will insert the teams with the platoon Sergeant. After the insertion he will receive

Realizing it is my choice and my choice alone to be a Reconnaissance Marine,
I accept all challenges involved with this profession.
Forever shall I strive to maintain the tremendous reputation of those who went before me.
Exceeding beyond the limitations set down by others shall be my goal.
Sacrificing personal comforts and dedicating myself to the completion of the reconnaissance mission shall be my life.
Physical fitness, mental attitude, and high ethics
The title of Recon Marine is my honor.
Conquering all obstacles, both large and small, I shall never quit.
To quit, to surrender, to give up is to fail.
To be a Recon Marine is to surpass failure;
To overcome, to adapt, and to do whatever it takes to complete the mission.
On the battlefield, as in all areas of life, I shall stand tall above the competition.
Through professional pride, integrity, and teamwork,
I shall be the example for all Marines to emulate.
Never shall I forget the principles I accepted to become a Recon Marine.
Honor, Perseverance, Spirit, and Heart.
A Recon Marine can speak without saying a word and achieve what others can only imagine.

Two Marines from 3rd Platoon, 2nd Force Recon Company head out for a raid against Al Qaeda forces near Khandahar. Force Recon has played an essential role in the current war against terrorism. *USMC Photo*

reports from the teams and report the situation on the ground to the supported commander. Officers only get into the fight during limited scale raids (Direct Action missions involving the MSPF element). It is possible for an Officer to lead a patrol, but not probable."

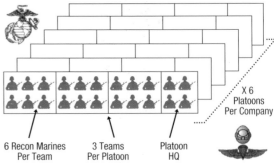

6 Recon Marines Per Team   3 Teams Per Platoon   Platoon HQ   X 6 Platoons Per Company

There are six platoons in each Force Reconnaissance Company. The platoons are broken down into three six-man teams and a HQ or Headquarters section.

Close Quarters Battle or CQB comes under the "Black Side." These Direct Actions missions would include such action as assaulting a radar station or terrorist training camp, or performing a VBSS or GOPLAT. During the operations, the Marines of Force Recon depend on their precision shooting skills.

Special Amphibious Reconnaissance Corpsman (SARC)

The Force Recon Company has medical and dive personnel assigned from the Navy. While Corpsmen have always served with the Marines, the SARC assigned to Force Recon are unique from their shipboard counterparts. The Special Amphibious Reconnaissance Corpsman goes through the same training the Marines in Force Recon go through, plus their own advanced Combat Trauma Training. When assigned to the platoons, they are part of the team, riflemen first, blending in with the Recon Marines. They are a hybrid, combining the skills of a Recon Marine with the expertise of a Corpsman.

(Note: The following SARC prerequisites, tests, and background are provided by Lieutenant Junior Grade Mike Kafka, deputy public affairs officer, Bureau of Medicine and Surgery, U.S. Navy.)

Prerequisites
Age: 28 or younger (waiverable; Rank- E-3 (Petty Officer Third Class) to E-6 (Petty Officer First Class)

US citizen and able to obtain a secret security clearance

No non-judicial punishment (NJP) within the last two years prior to application

No courts martial

Must be able to pass a diving medical exam, dive pressure test, physical screening, and interview

Physical screening and interview must be performed by a Reconnaissance Corpsman, SEAL or Navy 1st Class diver

Physical Screening Test

The Physical Screening Test consists of the following:

USMC Physical Fitness Test (PFT) completed with a score of at least 250

10-minute rest

500 meter swim in 14 minutes or less using the side- or breaststroke, then treading water for 30 minutes

"Dive Level Test" wearing battle dress uniforms (BDUs) or dungarees with boots or boondockers, consisting of a series of calisthenics for 2 minutes with a 2-minute rest between exercises. The minimum that must be performed are:

Pushups (42)

Sit-ups (50)

Flutter kicks (20)

Hello dollies (20)

Mountain climbers (20)

Eight-count body builders (20)

Four-mile forced march in 50 minutes or less wearing a 50-pound rucksack

Background and Training

The current program began in 1992 when the pipeline and the Navy Enlisted Classifications (8427-Fleet Marine Force [FMF] Reconnaissance Corpsman and 8403- Special Amphibious Reconnaissance Independent Duty Corpsman-the SARC) originated. Prior to this, Corpsmen who volunteered to serve with Marine Reconnaissance units were trained piece meal once they completed screening for whatever unit they went

to. The schools they usually attended were the USMC Amphibious Recon Course or a local Recon Indoctrination Program, which qualified them for the MOS of 0321, Reconnaissance Marine. Navy SCUBA school, Army Basic Airborne School and Navy Special Operations Technician training, a two-week course run by the SEALs which taught diving medicine and hyperbaric chamber operation. If they completed 0321 training, dive school and SOT school they were awarded the NEC 8492, which was also the NEC that SEAL corpsmen were awarded.

In the mid 1980s it was recognized that Recon teams needed a Recon-specific training pipeline. The result was the current NECs and training pipeline. It begins with the Field Medical Service School at Camp Pendleton or Camp Lejeune, where teams learn basic medical skills, as well as how to interface with Marine Corps units.

Next is the USMC Basic Reconnaissance Course, where the HM and his Marine classmates learn the basics of the Reconnaissance trade. Then comes the USMC combatant dive school in Panama City, where they learn open- and closed-circuit diving with an emphasis on insertion using closed-circuit diving rigs. The HM will then attend the Diving Medicine Course, also at Panama City, where they learn dive medicine and hyperbaric chamber operations. Next, they attend Army Basic Airborne Training at Fort Benning, GA.

The final course is the six-month Army Special Operations Combat Medic course at Fort Bragg, North Carolina. It focuses on trauma medicine and field medicine. During this course Corpsmen must pass the national registry paramedic test and then perform a month of clinical training with a large city's paramedic service. This training qualifies them for the NEC-8427. After serving and deploying for five years with the Marines for at least one Sea rotation, they may request training to become an 8403. Training for the 8403 NEC is the Army Advanced Special Operations Combat Medic course at Fort Bragg. This is the Medical training for Army Special Forces, and lasts approximately 12 months.

FMF Amphibious Reconnaissance Corpsman
Provides Medical and Operational services for FMF reconnaissance personnel engaged in amphibious reconnaissance & surveillance and other missions as directed by higher headquarters. Performs routine sick call, preventive medicine, Advanced Trauma Life Support (ATLS), Advance Cardiac Life Support (ACLS), minor surgical procedures, paramedic skills, and other routine and emergent procedures as required. Instructs and advises operational personnel in measures for prevention of illness and treatment of injuries associated with swimming, combat diving, military free fall, and amphibious operations. Assesses and treats diving related medical disorders. Trained in the operation of decompression chambers and as inside tender to care for patients suffering from diving related injuries or other conditions requiring hyperbaric medical treatment. Performs diving and airborne operations, in direct support of reconnaissance operations.

Special Amphibious Reconnaissance Independent Duty Corpsman
Performs duties as an HM 8427, as described above. Performs diagnostic patient care as well as associated operational, administrative, and logistical duties. Performs basic anesthesia, minor surgical, basic clinical laboratory, basic radiology, and other routine and emergency health care procedures as required. Instructs and advises junior medical and operational personnel in prevention and treatment of illness and injuries. Performs all patient care and medical management functions as set forth in chapter 9 of the Manual of the Medical Department (MANMED) operating independently of physicians and functions as health care providers.

When would a corpsman go out on patrol? Captain Christian explains, "We have one Corpsman [SARC] attached to most Platoons. The corpsman usually is attached out to one team for the duration of a mission. He has all of the same qualifications as a Force Recon Marine with additional Special Forces Medical training. We don't have enough to go out with every team, however, inside every Force Team you will find a school Trained EMT who is familiar with basic trauma care. The platoon Commander makes the call when the corpsman will be employed and with what team. Usually a Corpsman works with the same team for the duration of an 18-month float cycle."

Selection and Training

CHAPTER 4

Assignment to a Force Reconnaissance Company is an extensive and demanding process. The first step in this process is "selection." In order for a Marine to be considered for Recon he must be a U.S. citizen, volunteer, and be able to obtain a Secret Clearance. He must have a current physical, CWS-1 swimmer; 1st Class PFT (Marine Physical Fitness Test); and minimum GCT (Government Competitive Test) score of 105. Applicant must have 20/20 vision with minimum correction allowed, normal color vision, and good hearing. Any MOS (Military Occupational Specialties) may apply, though a high percentage of candidates come from infantry, scout/sniper, or Battalion Recon positions. A significant advantage in the selection process over other services is the fact that all Marines have attended Boot Camp and the School of Infantry. So, regardless of their MOS, they have experience with a rifle and land navigation and know how to patrol both day and night. This is contrary to BUD/S, for example, where incoming sailors have no experience with weapons. Recommended requirements include minimum rank of corporal with at least one deployment, high moral character, and high motivation. Finally, as Force Recon is a combat unit, it is limited to male Marines only.

Selection

Depending on the unit and manpower, Selection is run one day each month. It is designed to prepare the candidate for the "pipeline" of schools that a prospective Force Recon Marine would attend. While Selection may vary from unit to unit, the typical selection consists of the following: Testing begins early in the morning and runs well into the afternoon. It kicks off with the standard PFT, encompassing a three-mile run, sit-ups, and pull-ups. Next stop is the pool, where wearing "cammies" and boots they will perform water aerobics, underwater pushups, and swimming with "the brick," which involves retrieving a ten-pound brick from the water and swimming to the end of the pool. Passing the pool phase of selection is critical, as the water is a primary means of insertion for Force Recon. Next comes the level set, more calisthenics including pushups, pull-ups, flutter kicks, and eight-count body builders (a combination of squat thrust/pushups or other calisthenics of the instructors' choice). Enlisted men must score 275 (out of 300), and officers 285.

Then it is off to the Obstacle Course. The candidates will run the "O Course" twice, back to back. According to Staff Sergeant Joe Tablada, 4th Force Reconnaissance Company, "The instructors are looking for greatest attempt. Not just who finishes first, but who is putting out maximum effort." Following the Obstacle Course is the Ruck Run. Candidates are given a rucksack with a 50-pound sand bag and weapon (rubber duck) and head out for an eight-mile run. As they run, instructors admonish any stragglers to stay up with the pack or they are gone.

Each Marine has a member of the Unit monitoring him during each phase of the Selection. Although Marines must achieve high scores in all phases of the Selection in order to receive a passing mark, the final decision is up to the

Where it all begins: Amphibious Reconnaissance School (ARS). For East Coast Marines, they'll attend here at Fort Story, while West Coast Marines attend Basic Reconnaissance Course in Coronado. Same course, different names; it's an East Coast / West Coast Marine thing.

Force Recon Marines are taught how to perform a hydrographic survey of potential landing sites. These Marines in Okinawa are practicing these skills. The Recon men on shore are giving visual signals to fellow Marines in the water with the use of oars. *Defense Visual Information Center*

monitoring cadre that evaluated the Marine. The standards are not given out in order to ensure each Marine gives 110% the entire time. Candidates are not harassed or demeaned during the Selection process. Quitting during any phase of the Selection is allowed and does not disqualify a Marine from taking the Selection at a later date. It is not uncommon for a Marine not to pass the Selection on his first attempt. Often it takes a Marine three or four attempts through the process before he will succeed.

Upon successful completion of the physical test, the Marine undergoes a psychological screening and then an interview. For Officers, it is with the Company Commander. For enlisted Marines, it is with the Company Sergeant Major and other senior NCOs. They are looking for that highly motivated Marine: the guy who just won't quit and will drive on, no matter what the odds or circumstances.

Recon Indoc Platoon

The Reconnaissance Indoctrination Platoon or RIP is the next step for the potential Force Recon Marine. Progression to RIP will further refine the skills he needs for assignment to a Force Recon Company and ramps-up the candidate for Amphibious Reconnaissance School, or ARS. During RIP, attention will be given to Patrolling Techniques, Land Navigation, Amphibious Reconnaissance, and Communications. An interesting aspect of RIP entails each Marine being given a length of rope approximately 12 feet in length. It will be his constant companion and any time during training an instructor may request him to "Stop and tie me a prusik knot" or other knots of his choosing. So common is this practice that the RIP students are often referred to as "ropers." This program also serves as an extension of "Selection," weeding out the less motivated, and assuring that those who continue on with the "Recon Pipeline" have what it takes to carry out these hazardous missions. It has been compared by some Marines as Recon's version of "Hell Week," although RIP may last from three weeks to six months, depending on the openings in training or company billets.

It is worth noting that if a Marine is coming from Battalion Recon, he does not go through RIP. Rather, he will be assigned directly to a Force Recon Company, since he has already gone through the BRC.

Training Cycles

Force Reconnaissance training falls into two categories: Deep Reconnaissance (Green Side) and Direct Action (DA) (Black Side) missions. Each Force Recon Marine goes through a two year work-up cycle which includes: six months Individual Training Phase, six months Unit or Platoon Training Phase (Deep Reconnaissance), six-months MEU (SOC—Special Operations Capable) (Direct Action) Training Phase, and the six month MEU (SOC) Deployment. Upon return, the platoon has a

Recon School will teach the essential skills of small boat operations, such as nautical navigation, amphibious reconnaissance, and CRRC coxswain. *Defense Visual Information Center*

Post-deployment Phase, which can last three to six months. During this time the platoons prepare for their next work-up cycle.

The Individual Training Phase is when the Marines go to their specialized reconnaissance schools. Those Marines just beginning their tour with Force Recon will attend the Basic Reconnaissance Course, Airborne School, the Marine Combatant Diver School, and SERE (Survival, Evasion, Resistance and Escape) School. These schools will establish a basis upon which all other courses will be built.

Those Marines already qualified as Force Recon MOS will utilize this Individual Training Phase attending various schools to acquire additional advanced reconnaissance skills, such as Ranger, Pathfinder, Long Range Surveillance (LRS), Emergency Medical Technician (EMT), Military Freefall (MFF), and Static Line or MFF Jumpmaster schools. They may also attend schools in Applied Explosives, the Mountain Leaders Course (Winter and Summer), Helicopter Rope Suspension Training (HRST) Master, Scout/Sniper, and High Risk Personnel (HRP) Course.

Recon School

The training of Reconnaissance Marines is conducted at two locations and lasts for 56 days. The West Coast Marines attend the Basic Reconnaissance Course (BRC) located at the Naval Amphibious Base in Coronado, California, and the East Coast Marines are trained at the Amphibious Reconnaissance School (ARS) at Fort Story, Little Creek, Virginia. The school is open to all ranks from private to captain. However, to achieve the maturity level the cadre is looking for, the ideal candidate will be a corporal or sergeant with at least one deployment and a minimum of two years in service. While all Marines receive the fundamentals of scouting and patrolling at SOI, it is here at the BRC where those skills will be refined as he is taught those capabilities required to operate in the reconnaissance situation.

According to the BRC course description provided by Major D.S. Howe OIC, ARS, Ft. Story, "The course provides the student with a working knowledge of reconnaissance doctrine, concepts, and techniques with emphasis on ground and amphibious point and area amphibious reconnaissance missions. The course combines

Throughout Force Recon training, land navigation is emphasized. Although they may have a Global Positioning System device in their rucksack, they will turn to the time-honored practice of using a map and lensatic compass. Using a bearing or "dead reckoning," the Marines of Force Recon are masters of land navigation.

lecture, demonstration, and practical reconnaissance skills, patrolling, reconnaissance missions, nautical navigation, amphibious reconnaissance, technical reporting, CRRC coxswain, and physical training. Students must be capable of enduring long hours and a physically demanding course." The Basic Recon Course encompasses five core skills of the Reconnaissance Marine: Communications; Supporting Arms; Amphibious Recon; Land Navigation, and Ground Recon.

Communications

Trainees learn basic concepts in the establishment of communication nets, reporting procedures, and radio operation. Emphasis is given to long-range communication, high-gain antennas, and digital communication equipment. Emphasis of instruction is an ongoing and always changing process. For now the curriculum is the following: Radio Theory, Basic Radio Procedures, Communications Security (COMSEC), and Antenna Theory, including Field Expedient Antennas. Students will have exposure to an abundance of "comm" gear such as the: AN/PRC-119, AN/PRC-104, AN/PRC-113, AN/PSC-2 Digital Communication Terminal (DCT), AN/PRC-138 or 150, AN/PSN-11 (GPS), AN/PRC-148 (MBITR) and the AN/PRC-117.

Supporting Arms

In this phase of training the students will learn the fundamentals, principles, and techniques for interfacing with calling and adjusting Naval gunfire, artillery, close air support (CAS), and close-in fire support. The "Call for Fire" is a message prepared by the Recon team and contains information needed by the Fire Direction Center to determine the method of attack. Whether he is calling in an air strike from a "fast mover" or requesting CAS from a helicopter gunship, the Force Recon Marine will have the skill set to accurately prosecute his mission.

The last rays of the sun shine on the recon students as they fade into the woods. LCP Joel Wood of Class 0302 serves as rear guard for the team. Their mission is to perform a river reconnaissance to ascertain whether it is usable for follow-on forces. What the students do not know yet is that beavers have dammed the river and it is now a lake. ARS teaches not only the recon skills but also how to adapt to the situation.

Amphibious Recon

This phase of ARS will familiarize the students with the role of reconnaissance in an amphibious operation. They will learn everything there is about the F-470 Zodiac, also referred to as the Combat Rubber Raiding Craft or CRRC. They will practice surf passage to pilot the CRRC into and out of the surf zone. Further techniques are taught in methods of insertion, extraction, beach surveys, hydrographic surveys, reporting beach and surf conditions, and scout swimmer techniques.

Airborne training for Force Recon Marines is conducted at Fort Benning, Georgia. During these three weeks the Marines will learn the basic skills necessary to insert via parachute. After the successful completion of five jumps, they will receive their Silver Wings. To obtain their Gold Wings they will make an additional five jumps under USMC standards.

Land Navigation

During the Land Nav portion of the course, the future Force Recon Marines will learn the applied navigational techniques that will allow the team to traverse cross-country during day or night. They will become conversant with map and lensatic compass, and master Orientation, Pace Counting, Azimuths, Grid Coordinates and Global Positioning System (GPS). At the end of this training the student must pass a written exam, a night land navigation course (five nav points), and a day land navigation course (ten nav points).

Ground Recon
Patrolling

In this segment of training the Marines will receive an introduction to Reconnaissance Patrolling. They will learn Area and Zone Reconnaissance and Surveillance. The men will learn the organization and duties of team members. They will practice how to move day or night deep behind enemy lines, and how to conduct Immediate Action Drills (IAD) should they encounter an enemy force. Further instruction is given in camouflage and concealment. They will learn how to set up a Patrol Base, a Harbor Site, and a Communications Site. Special emphasis is given to the techniques used for observation post, helicopter landing zone, route, bridge, ford, and initial terminal guidance missions.

Reconnaissance Skills

Skills covered include field photography using regular camera and underwater cameras. Also covered are field sketching, range estimating, knots and rope management, and insertion/extraction techniques, including Rappelling, Fast Rope and the Special Patrol Insertion / Extraction System. Additionally, they will be trained on various observation devices, individual skills, and techniques for employment of explosives and claymore mines. During this phase they will also learn basic survival skills.

Upon successful completion of the nine-week course, the trainee will graduate BRC with the Primary MOS of 0321 Recon Marine. Worth noting is the fact that a career path has been established for these highly trained Marines.

Advanced schools include the Marine Corps Mountain Warfare Training Center, Bridgeport, California. The winter course will emphasize cold weather operations; while the summer course will concentrate on mountaineering skills, such as rock climbing and rappelling. Here, a pair of Marines put into practice these winter skills in the woods of Albania. *Courtesy 2nd Force Recon. USMC*

Previously, once a Force Recon Marine was through with his deployment he would be reassigned to another unit. Today, these Marines may now stay in the Force Recon community, honing warrior skills, learning new techniques, and developing their capabilities.

Combatant Diver Course

Next is the U.S. Marine Corps Combatant Diver Course at the Naval Diving and Salvage Training Center, Panama City, Florida. The eight-week course provides the Marines with combat underwater tactical swimming training. The Combatant Diver Course provides diver training through classroom instruction, extensive physical training, drown-proofing, pool familiarization dives, open water surface swims, and underwater infiltration swims with approximately 60% of the open water diving conducted at night. At the end of the course, the students

The Combatant Diver Course develops a highly confident and capable combat diver. The students are trained using the most current tactical doctrines and equipment. Emphasis is placed on developing in the student the skills and confidence required to successfully conduct an underwater infiltration and exfiltration. Here, an instructor harasses a student by simulating a "surf zone" tangle. The student must regain control of his equipment, and do so without panicking. Success of his insertion or extraction depends greatly on the Marine's abilities to be at home in the water. *Courtesy SSgt Joseph Tablada*

are assigned mission profiles where they are required to infiltrate underwater into their objective areas.

The course is designed to meet the needs of the Marine Corps in accordance with current Mission Performance and Training Standards. It is designed to provide qualified non-diving enlisted and officer personnel with the specialized training necessary to effectively operate as reconnaissance dive team members during underwater infiltration swims. Marines must arrive undetected, on target, while keeping team integrity and maintaining the ability to execute their assigned tasks on respective shore-based objectives.

The specific course prerequisite qualifications include the following: Individuals must be volunteers; Marines must be graduates of the Basic Reconnaissance Course; and candidates must successfully complete a physical fitness entry-level test within 30 days of reporting to the course; all personnel must possess an up-to-date diving physical examination. The age limit for the course is 35 years. The ASVB GT Score must be at least 100, and the candidate must have a minimum service of 12 months remaining upon completion of the course.

The Combatant Diver Course is 35 days in length. It is divided into four phases: Physical Conditioning, Combat Diver Principles and Fundamentals, USMC Open Circuit Diving Equipment and Operations, and USMC Closed Circuit Diving Equipment and Operations. The end of training is marked with the class, in four-to-eight-man reconnaissance teams, executing a field exercise that requires them to infiltrate surface and sub-surface, move to and conduct assigned missions on land, and extract from their assigned objective area. Upon successful completion of the training, the student is certified by the U.S. Navy and Marine Corps as a USMC Combatant Diver and has a Primary MOS of 8653.

Force Recon Marines may attend the U.S. Army Military Freefall Parachutist School, Ft. Bragg, North Carolina. Here, they will learn techniques and practice in the Vertical Wind Tunnel or VWT, which simulates the effects of free-falling at a speed of approximately 200 feet per second. The VWT generates winds up to 132 miles per hour, capable of supporting two jumpers with equipment up to 375 pounds. After ground week, students head out to Yuma Proving Grounds, Arizona. They begin training with jumps from 10,000 feet with no equipment, and work up to 25,000 feet with full equipment load and oxygen system. Each student will perform a minimum of 16 freefall jumps; this will include two day and two night jumps with oxygen and full field equipment. These jumpers are preparing for a night jump from a C-130 aircraft at 25,000 feet AGL. Standing in the rear of the aircraft they are still on the plane's oxygen lines. When ready, they will switch from the aircraft's oxygen console to their bailout bottles. *Courtesy 2nd Force Recon. USMC*

The Marines are known for producing some of the best riflemen in the world. At Scout/Sniper School, they make them better! The trainee will learn not only shooting skills, but also observation and surveillance techniques. Sniper Schools are at Camp Lejeune, North Carolina and Camp Pendleton, California; the Advance Sniper Course is at Quantico, Virginia. Shown here is a method of using the spotter's shoulder to stabilize the rifle. *Courtesy SSgt Joseph Tablada*

Parachute Training

For the next three weeks the Marines will be taught the basics needed to become "Airborne" qualified at the U.S. Army Airborne School, Ft. Benning, Georgia. They will learn the skills they will build upon to perform an insertion via parachute. Basic airborne training is broken into three weeks: Ground, Tower, and Jump Week.

Ground Week begins with an intensive program of instruction designed to prepare the Marine to complete his parachute jump. He will learn how to execute a Parachute Landing Fall (PLF) to land safely in the LZ. The Parachute Landing Fall consists of five points of contact designed to absorb the shock of landing and distribute it across the balls of the feet, calf, thigh, buttocks, and push-up muscle of the back. Using mockups of a C-130 and a C-141, they will learn the proper way to exit an aircraft.

Next comes Tower Week. Using a training device known as the swing-landing tower (SLT), the Marine is hooked up to a parachute harness, and he jumps from a 12-foot-high elevated platform. The apparatus provides the downward motion and oscillation simulating that of an actual parachute jump. To make things more challenging for the student, the instructors have control of the SLT and can determine if they want to land him hard or soft. During week two the student gets to ride the "Tower." The tower is designed to give the student practice in controlling their parachute during the descent from 250 feet, and execute a PLF upon landing.

Week three is Jump Week. The Recon Marine will perform five parachute jumps. First is an individual jump with a T-10B parachute. Next comes a mass exit with equipment and T-10B chute, then another individual exit with MC1-1B parachute and tactical assembly. His fourth jump will be a mass exit at night with T-10B and tactical equipment, and finally the fifth jump is either an individual jump with an MV1-1B or

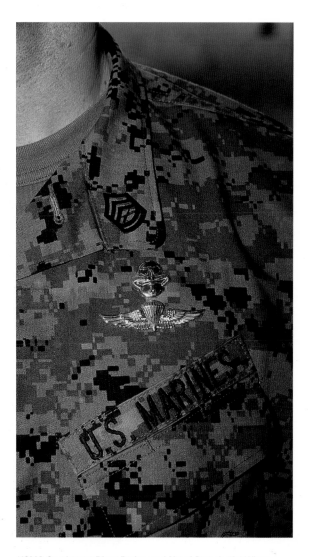

USMC Combatant Diver Badge and Naval Parachutist Wings, symbolic of insertion methods utilized by Force Recon. A Recon Marine who is both Parachute and SCUBA/UBA qualified will have the MOS 8654. The new Combatant Diver Badge, which is positioned at 1/8 inch above the wings, indicates the wearer is qualified on the LAR-V rebreather system. Marines who have not transitioned to the rebreather systems will still wear the basic SCUBA badge or "Bubble."

Explosive breaching is essential in "taking down" a building housing terrorists or other hostile targets. Here a member of 2nd Force Recon practices placing a breaching charge. The usage of these explosive methods aids in the Dynamic Entry of the MSPF during their assault. They will be instructed on a wide assortment of breaching methods, from taking out locks to reinforced steel doors. Nothing will stand in the way of a Marine and his mission. *Courtesy Force Recon Extreme Team*

mass jump with a T-10B parachute. Upon graduation he will be awarded the paratrooper Silver Wings and is now "Airborne" qualified.

Upon graduation from this course, his Primary MOS 8652 is now Reconnaissance Man, Parachute Qualified. At this point he wears the silver jump wings. To obtain the "Gold Wings" or Navy/Marine Parachutist badge, he must perform an additional five parachute jumps. These include a day and night "slick" jump, which is just with parachute and no equipment, and a day and night jump with full equipment. The fifth jump is usually a water jump. Note: the Primary MOS of a Force Recon Marine who is both Parachute and Combat Diver qualified is 8654.

Survival Evasion Resistance Escape School

The Force Recon Marines will receive instruction at the Survival Evasion Resistance Escape (SERE) School either at NAS North Island, California; or Camp McKall, North Carolina. Worth noting is that while each of these schools teach SERE, only the Camp McKall course is directed specifically for behind-the-lines operators. The other school is aimed at aviators. Basic SERE is designed to provide Level "C" Code of Conduct training to selected high-risk-of-capture personnel. Training is accomplished by providing basic skills necessary for world-wide survival, expediting search and rescue efforts, evading capture by hostile forces, resistance to interrogation, exploitation and indoctrination, and escape from detention when held by enemy forces. The course length is 12 days broken into three phases, phase one consisting of five-days of academic classroom, phase two consisting of six field laboratory days, and phase three consisting of debriefs and graduation. Course classification is *"CONFIDENTIAL."* Therefore, any student must possess a certification of CONFIDENTIAL or higher Security Clearance to attend the school. For reasons of

Located in a hanger at Wright Paterson AFB, the members of the MSPF of the 26th MEU(SOC) receive the final briefing during a TRUEX in Dayton, Ohio. Seen in nomex assault suits and gear are (l-r) GySgt Ed Lynch and Capt. Andy Christian of 6th Platoon, 2nd Force Recon Company, who will conduct the actual "hit" on the target. The other Marines are part of the security element or "trailers," who will provide cover for the assault team.

OPSEC, we will not expand on the lessons learned by the Marines at this school.

Additional survival training may include Peacetime Detention and Hostage Survival (PDAHS). The PDAHS course is designed to provide Level "C" Code of Conduct training to selected high-risk-of-capture personnel for peacetime hostile government detention and hostage

The usage of Simunitions increases the realism of training in a force-on-force, CQB, or other tactical scenarios. This M4 has been modified to use the marking cartridge ammunition, which uses a plastic sabot containing colored detergent (either red or blue). It launches the 0.5-gram projectile out of the muzzle at about 550 feet per second. The blue barrel on an M4 indicates it is set up for the Simunitions rounds. *USMC Photo*

survival. Training is provided in basic skills necessary for surviving peacetime hostile government/terrorist hostage captivity. This five day course is broken into two phases, phase one consisting of peacetime governmental detention, and phase two consisting of terrorist hostage survival. Course classification is *"SECRET,"* for which reason any student must have a certification of SECRET or higher Security Clearance. As is the SERE course, PDAHS is also taught at Camp Warner Springs, North Island, California.

The next six-month period is the Unit Training Phase. This is also referred to as the Platoon Work-up Phase and consists of the following training packages: Long Range Communications,

Advanced Parachute/HAHO, Amphibious Recon, Combat Dive, Weapons and Tactics, Combat Trauma, Desert Patrolling, Mountain Patrolling, and Long Range Patrols.

The third phase is the MEU(SOC) Training and is conducted by Special Operations Training Group, or SOTG. During this six-month segment, the Force Recon platoons will learn the "Black Side" or DA operations. They will have time in the "Shooting House" as Staff Sergeant Archer of SOTG relates, "You want to make sure that the people you want breathing come out breathing and that those you don't want breathing aren't." The SOTG courses will include: Explosive Breaching, Close Quarter Battle, Urban Reconnaissance & Surveillance, GOPLAT (Gas/Oil Platform) training, VBSS (Visit Board Search and Seizures), and shipboard assaults. During this phase the platoon will practice their newly acquired skills in TRUEX (Training in an Urban Environment) training packages. These and other mission-specific operations prepare the platoons for a wide assortment of missions aimed at supporting the MEU(SOC).

Training in an Urban Environment

The lessons learned by the U.S. military in such places as Kosovo, Haiti, and especially Somalia have brought the impact of urban combat to the forefront among Marine commanders. Fighting on a desolate desert plain, or isolated GOPLAT op is one thing, but when the mission calls for the entry into an urban environment, it's a whole new game. As was seen on numerous missions conducted by the U.S. Marines, the world is urbanizing and when trouble flares, these "hot" spots will place them in harm's way in a heartbeat. Commenting on this subject, Colonel Andrew P. Frick, Commanding Officer 26th MEU(SOC) relates, "In a rapidly urbanizing world, Marines of the 265th MEU must be prepared to meet any contingency–humanitarian assistance, peace-keeping or mid-intensity conflict, simultaneously, in a threeblock environment. It is only though realistic training that Marines will be prepared to meet these challenges and win."

This realistic training is the TRUEX where an average of 600 Marines, including support elements, descend on a city and conduct urban operations. The exercise is coordinated closely with local, state and federal officials, including the local police, fire department, the Federal Aviation Administration (FAA), and the Federal Bureau of Investigation (FBI). The TRUEX, or simply called "The True," has taken place in over 43 cities around the United States, such at Atlanta, New York, Miami, San Francisco, Charlotte, New Orleans, and Dayton. Such training allows MSPF to bring a fresh approach to every mission; after all, you can only run the MOUT site on-base so many times before you begin to know that the OpForce is waiting around that corner or this window. For the next two weeks CH-46s and CH-53s insert teams, Hueys perform MEDEVACs, and Cobras and Harriers provide CAS. Some of these missions are carried out within a stone's throw from residential neighborhoods and in dense downtown areas.

The culmination of third phase is the Special Operations Capable Exercise, or SOCEX, where all the members of the MEU(SOC) come together for a major exercise. The SOCEX must meet over 20 mission capabilities in order to be certified SOC and be considered ready to deploy. Upon successful certification the MEU(SOC) is ready for the forth phase, a Six-Month Deployment, or "Float" as it is often called. Those members of 1st Force Recon on the West Coast will deploy to the Persian Gulf area, while the members of 2nd Force Recon on the East Coast will deploy to the Mediterranean Sea. Upon returning from deployment, the work-up cycle begins, and the Marines of Force Recon start at the "Individual Phase" anew.

After the Company training phase, the Force Recon detachment is assigned via CHOP to SOTG for further training which will assist them in their role as MSPF for the MEU(SOC). During this six-month phase they will received training in CQB, Explosive Breaching, Urban Sniper, and Training in an Urban Environment or TRUEX. The training cycle culminates with a Special Operations Certification Exercise or SOCEX, which will certify the MEU as Special Operation Capable and ready for deployment. Here, Captain Andy Christian adjusts the FSBE on a fellow teammate prior to the exercise.

CHAPTER 5

Weapons

M4A1 Carbine Close Quarter Battle Weapon

Manufactured by Colt, the M4A1 is the Carbine version of the full size M16A2 assault rifle. This weapon was designed specifically for the U.S Special Operations Forces. For Force Recon Marines it is referred to as the Close Quarter Battle Weapon. The fire selector for the M4A1 can be set for semi- and full-automatic operation. The M4A1 is designed for speed of action and lightness of weight, as is often required by Force Recon shooters. The barrel has been redesigned to a shortened 14.5", which reduces the weight while maintaining its effectiveness for quick-handling operations in the field. The collapsible buttstock has four intermediate stops allowing adaptability in CQB without compromising shooting capabilities.

The M4A1 has a rifling twist of one in seven inches making it compatible with the full range of 5.56mm ammunitions. Its sighting system contains dual apertures, allowing for 0 to 200 meters, and a smaller opening for engaging targets at a longer range of 500 to 600 meters. Selective fire controls for the M4 have eliminated the three-round burst, replacing it with safe, semi-automatic, and full-automatic fire. There is also a detachable carrying handle, which when removed exposes a Weaver-type rail for mounting a SOPMOD accessories weapon, which is discussed below.

In addition to the CQB capabilities of the carbine, the M4A1 also provides the necessary firepower when targets must be engaged at greater ranges. In Operation Desert Storm certain

elements were equipped with some suppressed 9mm rifles while performing SR missions. When one of the teams was compromised and facing a rush of oncoming Iraqi soldiers and local nomads, it would be the M-16 and Carbines laying down a hail of 5.56mm rounds out to 400 to 600 meters that allowed the team the extra edge they needed to extract from a bad situation. The same line of reasoning holds fast from the Somali experience, where the M-16 Carbine proved to be more durable and versatile, and the 5.56mm ammunition more lethal, than the 9mm pistol round.

The M4A1 Carbine is a most capable and deadly weapon, suitable to any Force Recon mission. Further refinements were requested to make the weapon even more effective, whether in close-in engagements or against long-range targets. To accomplish this, USSOCOM and Crane Division, Naval Surface Warfare Center developed the Special Operations Peculiar Modification (SOPMOD) kit. Introduced in 1994, the SOPMOD kit is issued to all U.S. Special Operations Forces to expand on the capabilities and operation of the M4A1 Carbine. The kit includes an assortment of standardized, versatile weapons accessories to meet needs across Special Operations Forces mission scenarios. As the Force Recon Marines migrate from the M-16 to the M4A1, they also bring the modifications of the SOPMOD kit into their armory as well.

M203 Grenade Launcher

The Quick Attach/Detach M203 Mount and Leaf Sight when combined with the standard M203

This is my rifle. There are many like it, but this
one is mine.

My rifle is my best friend. It is my life. I must
master it as I must master my life.

My rifle, without me, is useless. Without my rifle,
I am useless. I must fire my rifle true. I must
shoot straighter than my enemy who is trying
to kill me. I must shoot him before he shoots
me. I will...

My rifle and myself know that what counts in this
war is not the rounds we fire, the noise of our
burst, nor the smoke we make. We know that
it is the hits that count. We will hit...

My rifle is human, even as I, because it is my life.
Thus, I will learn it as a brother. I will learn its
weaknesses, its strengths, its parts, its
accessories, its sights and its barrel. I will ever
guard it against the ravages of weather and
damage as I will ever guard my legs, my
arms, my eyes and my heart against damage. I
will keep my rifle clean and ready. We will
become part of each other. We will...

Before God, I swear this creed. My rifle and
myself are the defenders of my country.
We are the masters of our enemy. We are
the saviors of my life.

So be it, until victory is America's and there is no
enemy, but peace!

Grenade Launcher provides additional firepower
to the operator giving him both a point and area
engagement capability. The most commonly utilized ammunition, is the M406 40mm projectile,
includes High Explosive Dual Purpose, HEDP; this
grenade has a deadly radius of five meters and is
used as anti-personnel and anti-light-armor. Additional projectiles include M381 HE; M386 HE;
M397 Airburst; M397A1 Airburst; M433 High-
explosive dual purpose (HEDP), M441 HE, M576
Buckshot, M583A1 40mm WS PARA ILLUM, M585
White star cluster, M651 CS, M661 Green star cluster, M662 Red star cluster, M676 Yellow smoke
canopy, M680 White smoke canopy, M682 Red
smoke canopy, M713 Ground marker - Red, M715
Ground marker - Green, M716 Ground marker -
Yellow, M781 Practice, M918 Target Practice, M992
Infrared Illuminant Cartridge (IRIC), 40mm Non-
Lethal Round, 40mm Canister Round, and 40mm
Sponge Grenade.

The M433 multi-purpose grenade, in addition
to the fragmentation effects, is capable of penetrat-
ing steel armor plate up to two inches thick. Future
development in 40mm grenades will introduce
airburst capability which will provide increased
lethality and bursting radius through prefrag-
mented, programmable high explosives warheads.

The quick-attach M203 combines flexibility
and lethality to the individual weapon. Utilizing
multiple M203 setups allows concentrated fire by
bursting munitions which are extremely useful
in raids and ambushes, or in illuminating or
obscuring the target while simultaneously delivering continuous HEDP fire. The M203 Grenade
Leaf Sight attaches to the Rail Interface System
for fire control.

The receiver of the M203 is manufactured of
high-strength forged aluminum alloy. This
provides extreme ruggedness, while keeping
weight to a minimum. A complete self-cocking
firing mechanism, including striker, trigger, and
positive safety lever, is included in the receiver.

The M4A1 Close Quarter Battle Weapon is a compact version of the full-sized M16A2 rifle. The M4A1 has a fire selection for semi- and full-automatic operation. The barrel has been redesigned to a shortened 14.5 inch, which reduces the weight, while maintaining its effectiveness for quick handling field operations in addition to the CQB capabilities of the Carbine, the M4A1 also provides the necessary firepower when targets must be engaged at greater ranges. This is one of the reasons the M4A1 has replaced the MP5 for CQB.

The M203 grenade launcher is a lightweight, single-shot, breech-loaded 40mm weapon specifically designed for placement beneath the barrel of the M4A1 Carbine. With a quick release mechanism, the addition of the M203 to the M4A1 Carbine creates the versatility of a weapon system capable of firing both 5.56mm ammunition as well as an expansive range of 40mm high explosive and special purpose munitions.

This will allow the M203 to be operated as an independent weapon, even though attached to the M16A1 and M16A2 Rifles and M4A1 Carbine. The barrel is also made of high-strength aluminum alloy, which has been shortened from 12 to 9 inches, allowing improved balance and handling. It slides forward in the receiver to accept a round of ammunition, then slides backward to automatically lock in the closed position, ready to fire.

Carrying out their missions in small teams, Force Recon Marines depend on rapid deployment, mobility, and increased firepower; where the emphasis is focused on "get in and get out" fast. The addition of the M203 brings the added firepower to the already proven and outstanding M4A1 Carbine.

M4A1 Accessory Kit
Rail Accessory System (RAS)

The Rail Accessory System (RAS) is a notched rail system, which replaces the front hand guards on the M4A1 receiver. This is similar to the SOP-MOD Rail Interface Systems or RIS. This rail system is located on the top, bottom and sides of the barrel, and facilitates the attaching of SOPMOD kit components on any of the four sides. The notches are numbered making it possible to attach the various components at the same position each time they are mounted. Optical sights and Night Vision Devices can be mounted on the top, while top and side rails would be the choice for positioning laser aiming devices or lights. The bottom of the RAS normally will accommodate the vertical grip and/or lights. When no accessories are mounted to the RAS, plastic hand guards are installed to cover and protect the unused portions of the rail.

This photo offers a good look at the Rail Attachment System or RAS. The RAS, manufactured by Knights Armament Company, allows the Force Recon Marines to affix an assortment of optics, laser, light, and other options to the weapon, depending on the mission.

The Trijicon Reflex Sight is a reflex collimator sight designed for Close Quarters Battle (CQB). The Reflex sight features an amber reticle that glows more or less brightly dependent on the ambient light conditions. One of the benefits of the Trijicon Reflex is that the unit operates without batteries.

A Force Recon Marine armed with an M4A1 sends a burst of 5.56mm rounds down-range in Khandahar, Afghanistan. His weapon is fitted with a peephole sight, which is lined up with the Reflex gunsight. Note: he has two of the 30-round magazines affixed together with "100 mile-per-hour tape." The pouches on his belt are for M249 SAW ammo boxes, but this Marine has adapted them to transport a number of M4 magazines to the range. *USMC Photo*

Optics
Reflex II

The Trijicon Reflex Sight is a reflex collimator sight designed for Close Quarters Battle (CQB). The Reflex sight provides a fast method of acquiring and hitting close and moving targets, as well as engaging targets while moving. The sight utilizes a tritium-illuminated dot usable for low light and nighttime use. Effective out to 300 meters, the Reflex Sight is optimized for speed and accuracy in close-range engagements (<50m) and close combat (<200m), providing the operator a heads-up fire control during both day and night, and with night vision equipment. The Reflex Sight can be utilized with either night vision goggles or in combination with a night vision monocular, such as the AN/PVS-14; this arrangement provides a lightweight day/night capability

The Aimpoint Comp-M sight superimposes a red dot on the target, allowing the Marine to make rapid sighting adjustments. The Comp-M is parallax free, which means the shooter does not have to compensate for parallax deviation, which is beneficial in the fas-tpaced shooting environment of CQB.

without having to rezero during the transition between day and night sights.

Aimpoint Comp-M

The Aimpoint Comp-M is used for CQB activities and is currently being fielded with Force Recon Companies as a replacement for the Reflex II. Using both eyes-open and heads-up method, the Marine is able to acquire the target with exceptional speed and precision. The Comp-M sight superimposes a red dot on the target which the brain sees, allowing the shooter to adjust his weapon according when required in the fast-pace shooting environment of CQB. The Comp-M is parallax free, which means the shooter does not have to compensate for parallax deviation. The sight may be mounted on the carrying handle or RAS of the M4A1.

AN/PAS-13 (V2)

Thermal Weapons Sight is capable of detecting targets in total darkness, in adverse weather, and through other combat environment obscurities, such as dust and smoke. Placing your eye on the sight and applying slight pressure activates the TWS, enabling the operator to detect personnel out to 1.5 kilometers and vehicles out to 4.2 kilometers. The TWS requires no visible light source to operate and can be used either as a weapon-mounted sight or hand-held imager. The AN/PAS-13 IR sensor receives infrared light, which in turn converts it into digital data. It is then processed and displayed digitally as an infrared image for the operator.

AN/PVS-17

The AN/PVS-17 is a lightweight, compact, night vision sight that provides the operator the capability to locate, identify, and engage targets from 20 to 300 meters. The MNVS features a wide field-of-view, magnified night vision image, and illuminated reticle; it is adjustable for windage

AN/PAS-13 (V2) Thermal Weapons Sight is capable of detecting targets in total darkness, in adverse weather, and through other combat environment obscurities, such as dust and smoke. Placing your eye on the sight and applying slight pressure activates the TWS, enabling the operator to detect personnel out to 1.5 kilometers and vehicles out to 4.2 kilometers. The TWS requires no visible light source to operate and can be used either as a weapon-mounted sight or hand-held imager.

and elevation. It can be hand held, or mounted on the weapon.

Lasers

AN/PEQ-2 Infrared Pointed Illuminator/Aiming Laser

The AN/PEQ-2 Infrared Target Pointer/ Illuminator/Aiming Laser (ITPIAL) allows the M4A1 to be effectively employed to 300 meters with standard issue night vision goggles (NVG) or a weapon-mounted night vision device, such as the AN/PVS-14. The IR illuminator broadens the capabilities of the NVGs in buildings, tunnels, jungle, overcast, and other low-light conditions where starlight would not be sufficient to support night vision. It also allows

The AN/PVS-17 Night Vision Sight is a replacement for the PVS-4. This sight incorporates the new Gen III image intensification I2 tube. It has a mounting attachment to interface with the Mil-std 1913 rail (RAS). The system weighs less than two pounds, contains a Mil-Dot reticle, and can be configured for either 2.25x or 4.5x magnification.

The AN/PEQ-2 Infrared Target Pointer/Illuminator/Aiming Laser (ITPIAL) allows the M4A1 to be effectively employed to 300 meters with standard issue night vision goggles (NVG) or a weapon-mounted night vision device, such as an AN/PVS-14. The ITPIAL is a dual-beam IR laser device, either handheld or weapon-mounted. There are seven modes of operation for aiming light and pointer/illuminator functioning individually or in combination, as well as high and low in aiming light power. The unit is waterproof down to two atmospheres.

Along with optics and IR laser, the Force Recon Marines will utilize white light. Here a SureFire light has been affixed to the M4A1. Visible white light provides illumination to facilitate moving inside darkened buildings, bunkers, tunnels, and so forth. The white light is useful for searching and identification of the target. The intense white light can also overwhelm an enemy in CQB, giving the operator the momentary advantage. There is also an IR cover for the light.

visibility in areas normally in shadow. At close range, a neutral density filter is used to eliminate flare around the aiming laser for improving the view of the target, for identification, as well as precision aiming. This combination provides the operator a decisive advantage over an opposing force with little or no night vision capability.

Other Accessories
Back-up Iron Sight (BIS)

The Back-up Iron Sight (BIS) provides the aiming ability similar to the standard iron sight on the carbine to 300 meters. The BIS may be used in conjunction with the Aimpoint sights and folds out of the way to allow the Day Optical Scope or Reflex Sight and night vision device to be mounted on the M4A1 Carbine. In the event the optical scopes are damaged or otherwise rendered inoperable, they can be removed and the BIS will then be used to complete the mission. The sight can also be used to bore-sight or confirm zero on the Reflex Sight or Visible Laser.

Forward Handgrip

The Forward or Vertical Handgrip, unofficially referred to as the "broom handle," attaches to the bottom of the RAS and provides added support, giving the operator a more stable firing platform. It can be used as a monopod in a supported position and allows the operator to hold the weapon despite overheating. The Forward Hand-grip can be used to push against the assault sling and stabilize the weapon with isometric tension during CQB. Using the handgrip brings the shooter's elbows in closer or tighter to his body, consequently keeping the weapon in front of the operator. The vertical handgrip also enables quicker handling when the additional components have been attached to the weapon, thus providing more precise target acquisition.

One of the drawbacks of the vertical grip is the possibility of the grip catching on a ledge or edge of the helicopter during egress or extraction. This issue is being addressed by the evaluation of a quick release lever on the forward grip. Some of the Force Recon Marines we talked with like the option, while others prefer using the carbine in the manner they were taught, sans the handgrip.

Quick Attach Suppressor

The Quick Attach/Detach Sound Suppressor Kit Mk4 MOD0 (QAD Suppressor) can quickly be attached to or removed from the M4A1 Carbine. With the suppressor in place, the report of the weapon is reduced by a minimum of 28 decibels (dB). As the 5.56mm round is supersonic, you will hear the bang, but it is more like a .22 caliber pistol than a 5.56mm round. With the suppressor attached, it buys some time, while the bad guys are trying to figure out, "What was that? Where did it come from?" By the time they figure out what is going on, the assault team should be in control of the situation.

The suppressor will also keep the muzzle blast to a minimum, assisting the entry team in situation awareness. While the suppressor does not completely eliminate the sound, it does reduce the firing signature of the flash and muzzle blasts. Using the suppressor is effective as a deceptive measure, interfering with the enemy's ability to locate the shooter and take immediate action. Additionally, it reduces the need for hearing pro-

tection during CQB engagements, thus improving inter-team voice communication.

Combat Sling

The Combat Sling affords a hassle-free, immediate, and secure technique for carrying the M4A1 Carbine, especially when equipped with assorted accessories from the kit. The Combat Sling can be used alone or with the mounting hardware to provide safe and ready cross-body carry or a patrol carry. Whether moving in close quarters in a close column formation or stack, the muzzle of the weapon is kept under control and does not sweep the operator or his teammates around him. The weapon is carried in a ready position to immediately engage hostile targets. Although issued with

A Quick Attach/Detach Sound Suppressor Kit can quickly be attached or removed from the M4A1 Carbine. With the suppressor in place the report of the weapon is reduced by a minimum of 28 decibels (dB). The suppressor also substantially reduces muzzle flash and blast. Note also a good view of the vertical handgrip or "broom handle" attached to the RAS.

The "combat accuratized" MEU(SOC) 45 is a modified M1911A1 .45-caliber pistol. Each pistol is hand-built by specially-trained armorers at the Rifle Team Equipment (RTE) shop in Quantico, Virginia. Here, the base weapon is upgraded and customized until it is a "match" grade precision handgun. The MEU(SOC) 45 is carried as a backup or secondary weapon, dependent on the mission. Here a CQB operator has transitioned from his M4A1 to the .45 caliber handgun. Switching over to the secondary could be due to an out-of-ammunition condition or malfunction of the primary weapon.

The Joint Service Combat Shotgun manufactured by Benelli is a gas-operated shotgun. While this would rarely, if ever, be used on Green Side ops, it does come in handy during Black Side missions, such as VBSS or GOPLAT operations. It is fitted with a collapsible stock, ghost ring sights, and a MilStdl9l3 rail on the receiver to facilitate the addition of optics, lasers, or lights.

the SOPMOD kit, various commercial manufacturers produce similar weapon slings as well as those worked up by the company riggers, which have also found their way into the kit bags of the Force Recon Marines.

MEU(SOC) 45

This weapon is a modified M1911A1 .45-caliber pistol sometimes referred to as "near match" or "combat accuratized." The MEU(SOC) Pistol is the designated backup or secondary weapon of Marines in CQB operations. The M1911A1 was chosen for this role (and its modifications generated) because of its inherent reliability and lethality, and because the MEU(SOC) modifications make the M1911A1 design more "user friendly."

The MEU(SOC) pistol has a number of unique characteristics. They feature a U.S. GI frame from such manufacturers as Colt, Remington Rand, Ithaca, or US&S; commercial slide from either Springfield Armory or Caspian ArmsSights custom-made by PWS; and Bar-Sto barrel and bushing. (Bar-Sto barrels have been used exclusively by the U.S. Marine Corps Marksman Unit since 1977.) All barrels have a rate of twist of 1 turn in 16 inches, resulting in an accuracy of 2 inches max at 25 yards using match-grade ammo. The MEU(SOC) pistol has King's Gun Works extra-wide grip safety for increased comfort and controllability (which aids in a quick follow-up second shot) and ambidextrous thumb safety lock; Videki long aluminum trigger Pachmayr rubber wrap-around grip panels; and high-profile combat sights. The issue magazines are replaced with Wilson Combat stainless steel; seven round competition-grade magazines with rounded plastic follower and extended floor plate. The weapon modifications were designed in 1986 to meet the requirements of the MEU(SOC). Each pistol is hand-built by specially trained armorers at the Rifle Team Equipment (RTE) shop in Quantico, Virginia. A recent modification after testing at the Marine Corps Systems Command, Raids and Recon, in Quantico has been the addition of a small bracket beneath the barrel on the receiver, which allows the attaching of a visible-light or laser-aiming device.

M-249SPW

The M249SPW or Special Purpose Weapon, (referred to as the ParaSAW), was developed by FN as the M249SPW, to meet the requirement for a lightweight variant of the standard M249, while retaining the intrinsic functionality and reliability of the weapon. The modification resulted in a reduction in weight of 4.1 pounds, as well as a new shortened lightweight barrel of 13.5 inches. The carrying handle and mounting lugs (for vehicular operations) have been removed.

The weapon is an individually portable, gas-operated magazine or disintegrating metallic link-belt fed, light machine gun with fixed headspace and quick-change barrel feature. The M249SPW can engage point targets out to 800 meters, firing the improved NATO standard 5.56mm cartridge. The SAW forms the basis of firepower for the fire team. The gunner has the option of using 30-round M-16 magazines or linked ammunition from pre-loaded 200-round plastic magazines. The gunner's basic load is 600 rounds of linked ammunition. The weapon weighs in at 19.30 pounds with a loaded 200 round linked ammunition magazine. Overall length is 35.75 inches buttstock extended, and 30.50 inches with the buttstock retracted.

During a patrol stop the Recon team's SAW gunner watches over his sector while the team leader calls in a SitRep. The M249 Para-SAW uses the same 5.56mm round as the M4A1; thus the team will not have to worry about carrying an assortment of ammunition. It is fitted with a 200-round magazine of linked 5.56mm ammo, with every fourth round a tracer, as can be seen by the orange tip. The M249 is an excellent weapon for laying down suppressive fire, and can easily be fired from the shoulder for accurate shot placement when needed.

M240G Medium Machine Gun

In an effort to replace their aging stock of 7.62mm machines guns, the U.S. Marines selected the M240G medium machine gun as a replacement for the M60 family of machine guns. Manufactured by Fabrique Nationale, the 24.2-pound M240B medium machine gun is a gas-operated, air-cooled, linked belt-fed weapon that fires the 7.62 x 51mm round. The weapon fires from an open-bolt position with a maximum effective range of 3725 meters. The cyclic rate of fire is 750 rounds per minute [low rate] and 950 rounds per minute [high rate] through an adjustable gas regulator. It features a folding bipod which attaches to the receiver, a quick-change barrel assembly, a feed cover and bolt assembly enabling closure of the cover regardless of bolt position, a plastic buttstock, and an integral optical sight rail. While it possesses many of the same characteristics as the older M60, the durability of the M240G system results in superior reliability and maintainability.

M40A1 Sniper Rifle

The M40A1 was put into service in the 1970s to meet the need of a long-range sniper rifle. Each rifle is hand built by specially trained and qualified personnel at the Marine Corps Marksmanship Training Unit (MTU) at Quantico, Virginia. The M40A1 Sniper Rifle is based on the Remington Model 700, a heavy-barrel, bolt-action, five-round magazine-fed 7.62mm rifle optimized for accuracy with match-grade ammunition. The weapon is equipped with a special Unertl 10-power sniper scope. With scope, the rifle weighs approximately 14.5 pounds. The unique characteristics of the M40A1 Sniper Rifle are: commercial competition-grade heavy barrel, McMillan fiberglass stock and

The M249 ParaSAW has been modified with a Rail Attachment System, allowing the attachment of SOPMOD kit accessories, i.e., optical sights, night vision devices, laser designators, IR aiming devices, flashlights and a forward pistol grip or bipod. The ParaSAW is an air-cooled, belt-fed, gas-operated automatic weapon that fires from the open-bolt position. It has a cyclic rate of 750 rounds per minute [rpm]. This M249 is fitted with an AN/PVS-14 Night Vision Optic and in this case a 30-round M-16 magazine is in place rather than the 200-round box magazine.

The M240G Machine Gun is the ground version of the original M240/M240E1, 7.62mm medium-class weapon manufactured by Fabrique Nationale and designed as a coaxial/pintle-mounted machine gun for tanks and light armored vehicles. The M240G in use with Force Recon has been modified for ground use by the installation of a flash suppressor, front sight, carrying handle for the barrel, a buttstock, infantry-length pistol grip, bipod, and rear-sight assembly.

The M40A1 has been the standard sniper rifle since 1976. It is 44 inches long and weighs approximately 15 pounds. The stock is from McMillan with a free-floating barrel, which is 6 groove, 1/12 twist, and 24 inches long. GySgt Ed Lynch of 2nd Force Recon engages a target during a training exercise in Israel. *Courtesy 2nd Force Recon*

butt pad, modified Winchester Model 70 floorplate and trigger guard, and modified and lightened trigger. In addition, each stock is epoxy bedded for accuracy, and all weapons must shoot less than one minute of angle (MOA).

M40A3

In 1996 the USMC armorers at Quantico began to design the replacement for the M40A1; the result was the M40A3. It uses a Remington 700 short action, chambered for 7.62mm NATO, with a steel floor plate assembly and trigger guard built by D. D. Ross. The barrel is Schneider Match Grade SS#7 and is 24 inches in length. The Unertl rings and bases have been replaced with D. D. Ross base and G&G Machine rings. The rifles also come with a Harris bipod and an accessory rail, also built by G&G Machine. The stock is a new McMillan Tactical A4, with adjustable cheek and length of pull.

As the older M40A1s rotate for service and repair, they are replaced by M40A3s. The rifles are extremely accurate, very rugged, and are designed from the ground up to be a superb sniper rifle. Combined with the new M118LR ammo, it makes a system that is ranked with the best in the world. The magazine capacity for the rifle is five rounds; it has an effective range of 1000 yards.

The M40A3 is the newest versions of the USMC sniper rifle. The rifles are extremely accurate, very rugged, and are designed from the ground up by USMC armorers at Quantico, Virginia, to be a superb sniper rifle. Worth noting is the new "Pixel" camouflage being worn by the Sgt Major.

Taking the "One Shot, One Kill" methodology to a higher level, Sgt. Xavier Lendof of 6th Platoon, 2nd Force Recon Company takes aim with the Barrett M82A1 .50-caliber semi-automatic rifle, also called the Special Application Scoped Rifle (SASR). This rifle can give the Force Recon team that added edge in a firefight as a covering or suppression weapon. It is capable of destroying light-skinned vehicles well out to 1500 meters and beyond. The SASR is designed to provide the MEU(SOC) commander the tactical option of employing snipers with anti-material capabilities, such as generators, bunkers, aircraft, and vehicles.

M-14 DMR Designate Marksman Rifle

The DMR is a precision grade, 7.62mm, semi-automatic rifle. It is equipped with a simple mounting system which will accommodate a day optical sighting scope, the AN/PVS-4 Starlight Scope, and other night/low-level target engagement equipment. The DMR also features an operator-attachable flash suppressor and uses both 10 and 20-round magazines. The "basic" DMR (minus the sight, magazine, sling, basic issue items, cleaning gear, suppressor, and bipod) weighs approximately 11 pounds. Marine Corps Scout/Sniper teams will employ the DMR when the mission requirements dictate the need for a weapon capable of delivering rapid, accurate fire against multiple targets at ranges out to 800 meters and with greater lethality than the M16A2 or M4A1 Carbine.

The Designated Marksman Rifle or DMR is based on the M-14 rifle system. It is shown here with the AN/PVS-10 gun sight. This rifle is also fitted with a sound suppressor. The spotter or backup sniper would most likely use this weapon. It could also be employed when the mission requires engaging multiple targets in rapid succession. *USMC Photo*

M82A1A .50 Caliber Special Application Scoped Rifle (SASR)

The M82A1A is a semi-automatic, air cooled, box-magazine-fed rifle chambered for the .50 caliber, M2 Browning Machine Gun cartridge. This rifle operates by means of the short recoil principle. The weapon system comprises the rifle (M82A1A) with a Unertl 10-power scope and an additional box magazine. The system comes packed in a watertight, airtight carrying case allowing the weapon to be carried through or under the water. The basic M82A1A rifle is equipped with bipod, muzzle brake, carrying handle, metallic

sights, and 10-round box magazine. There is also a backpack for cross-country transport, and a bandolier for extra magazines is available.

The M82A1A is designed to give commanders the tactical choice of employing snipers with an anti-material weapon to augment the present anti-personnel M40A1 or M40A3 7.62mm rifles. Barrett Firearms Manufacturing of Murfreesboro, Tennessee, manufactures the rifle. The scope is manufactured by Unertl to match the trajectory of the .50-caliber Raufoss Grade A, which is the standard operational round.

CHAPTER 6

Equipment

Communications

Communications or Comm is the lifeline of any Force Recon team on a mission. For deep reconnaissance and long-range communications, these "High Speed" Leathernecks have an assortment of communications equipment at their disposal. Comm gear is invaluable for calling SitReps (Situation Reports), sending back real-time imagery, or calling in CAS; it allows the Force Recon Marines to prosecute the mission to the max. During DA or CQB, the capability of inter/intra team radio communications is essential to the success of the operation.

The Raytheon AN/PRC-113 provides a lightweight, manpack radio with improved communications when co-located with other radios, due to its reduced transmitter noise floor and greater receiver range. The radio fully complies with Military Specifications, including Environment, EMI/EMC, TEMPEST, Nuclear Reliability, Maintainability and Human Factors. The PRC-113 is baseband COMSEC (Communication Security) compatible and is available with integral ECCM (Electronic Counter-Countermeasures).

The AN/PRC-117F covers the entire 30- to 512- MHz frequency range while offering embedded COMSEC and Havequick I/II ECCM capabilities. This advanced-software reprogrammable digital radio supports continuous operation across the 90 to 420 MHz band providing 20 W FM and 10 W AM transmit power with Havequick I/II capability (10 W FM in other frequency ranges).

The AN/PRC-117F supports a KY-57/VINSON compatible interface to ease backwards interoperability with fielded equipment. The radio also supports both DS-101 and DS-102 fill interfaces and all common fill devices for Havequick Word-of-Day (WOD) and encryption key information.

The AN/PRC-138 is the manpack companion to the RF-5000 FALCON™ Series Transceiver Systems. Capabilities and options are virtually identical. The AN/PRC-138 will interoperate with any RF-5000 Series equipment using ECCM, Automatic Link Establishment (ALE), voice, data, digital voice, or encryption. The AN/PRC-138 is a full-capability HF-SSB/VHF-FM transceiver that covers the 1.6 to 60 MHz spectrums in 10 Hz steps, providing the capabilities of an HF and a VHF radio in one small package.

AN/PRC-150

The AN/PRC-150 manufactured by Harris is an advance HF-SSB/VHF-FM man-portable tactical radio system. This multi-band system provides the Force Recon teams with a long-range and secure communication device. The AN/PRC-150 provides U.S. Type 1 voice and data encryption compatible with current cryptograph devices already in use with the Marines. Further COMSEC is achieved by the employment of ECCM providing reliable and secure HF communications. The keyboard/display can be removed for easy access to the controls.

DCT

Data Communication Terminal (AN/PSC-2), or DCT, is a handheld manpack digital communication computer that interfaces with a variety of tactical HF/VHF/UHF radio equipment, allowing for the capability to compose, edit, store, display,

Communications is the lifeline of the Force Recon Marines, although the methods have changed from World War II, when recon teams would perform their missions often armed with only a Ka-Bar knife, a pencil, and slate. Here, the recon team has stopped so the Team Leader can radio in a SitRep, which is set up in SatCom mode. Though the technology has modernized the process, the mission remains unchanged: get the information and report back to the commander.

The AN/PRC-113 is a portable, two band (VHF/UHF) receiver-transmitter. It is designed for short-range tactical ground-to-ground and ground-to-air communication. It can be used in conjunction with the KY-57/TSEC speech security equipment for secure voice communications.

transmit, and receive preformatted messages, free text messages, and graphics data. The DCT provides digital data communications via a burst transmission capability, thus making it a highly desirable and preferred means of communication in a high-threat environment by minimizing vulnerability to enemy radio direction finding and jamming. The DCT is employed to facilitate the exchange of tactical command and control messages for the purposes of close air support, fire support, anti-air defense, reconnaissance team reporting, and infantry unit control. The DCT is also used to transmit/record traffic as well as a general-purpose communication device.

AN/PRC-148 (V)

For tactical intra-team communications, the teams will be issued the Maritime Multi-Band Inter/Intra Team Radio. This provides the teams with the ability to communicate on user-selected frequency from 30 to 512 MHz utilizing a single hand-held radio, with power up to five watts in VHF/FM, VHF/AM, UHF/AM, UHF/FM(LOS) for ground-to-ground and air-to-ground connectivity. Weighing only 31 ounces, there are two versions immersable to six feet and 66 feet. The units are embedded COMSEC (Communications Security) for full digital voice and data operations.

Thales Communication Maritime Multiband Inter/Intra Team Radio (MBITR) is a powerful tactical handheld radio designed for the U.S. Special Operations Command. The MBITR more than met the tough SOCOM requirements and provides a secure voice and digital-data radio with exceptional versatility, ruggedness and reliability. The immersable unit weighs less than two pounds and includes a keypad, graphics display and built-in speaker-microphone. Typical of the advanced designs of Thales radios, MBITR utilizes digital-signal processing and flash memory to support functions traditionally performed by discrete hardware in other manufacturers' equipment. The power output is up to 5 watts over the 30- to 512-MHz frequency band. The MBITR has embedded Type 1 COMSEC for both voice and data traffic.

Global Positioning System (GPS)

While all Force Recon Marines excel in land navigation using the standard issue lensatic compass, it is equally important for the teams to be able to have pinpoint accuracy when conducting a DA mission through the desert, or across the frozen tundra, in enemy territory, or in the middle of the night. For such instances they will utilize a device known as Global Positioning System or GPS. Using a GPS receiver, the Marines pinpoint their exact location anywhere on the Earth.

Developed in the early 1970s by the U.S. Department of Defense, the Global Positioning System provides a continuous, worldwide positioning and navigational system for U.S.

Since communication is a hallmark of a Force Reconnaissance mission, it is imperative that any information is relayed in a clear and concise form. The phonetic alphabet was designed to allow clarity in communications when speaking over a radio or field phone. Due to vexing radio static or the tremendous background noise found in combat, early communicators found it difficult to distinguish between letters which may rhyme or sound similar. Thus, the phonetic alphabet was established to avoid confusion between, say, a "B" and a "D" when spelling or using letters of the alphabet. The phonetic alphabet has evolved since its inception, and has now been standardized internationally.

A	ALPHA	N	NOVEMBER
B	BRAVO	O	OSCAR
C	CHARLIE	P	PAPA
D	DELTA	Q	QUEBEC
E	ECHO	R	ROMEO
F	FOXTROT	S	SIERRA
G	GOLF	T	TANGO
H	HOTEL	U	UNIFORM
I	INDIA	V	VICTOR
J	JULIET	W	WHISKEY
K	KILO	X	X-RAY
L	LIMA	Y	YANKEE
M	MIKE	Z	ZULU

military forces around the globe. The complete constellation, as it is referred to, consists of 24 satellites orbiting approximately 12,000 miles above the Earth. These 22 active and two reserve or backup satellites provide data 24 hours a day for 2D and 3D positioning anywhere on the planet. Each satellite constantly broadcasts the precise time and location data. Troops using a GPS receiver receive these signals.

By measuring the time interval of the transmission and the receiving of the satellite signal, the GPS receiver calculates the distance between the users and each satellite. Using the distance measurements of at least three satellites in an algorithm computation, the GPS receiver provides the precise location. Using a special encryption signal results in Precise Positioning Service (PPS), which is used by the military. A

The multi-band AN/PRC-117F operates in VHF AM and FM, UHF AM, and UHF DAMA SATCOM. DAMA or Demand Assigned Multiple Access, permits several hundred users to share one narrowband SATCOM channel based on need or demand. It is voice/data and has embedded Crypto, SATCOM and ECCM capabilities. The AN/PRC-117F has a removable keypad allowing the RTO to control the radio's parameters while it is being carried on his back. The radio weighs 15.9 pounds with batteries and is 3.2 inches high x 10.5 inches wide x 13.5 inches deep. There is a GPS interface capability embedded which will transmit the user's coordinate when the operator keys the handset.

The AN/PRC-138 is a manpack radio operating in AM, USB, LSB, CW and FM modes. The radio can be password protected to prevent unauthorized usage. The AN/PRC-138 features Robust Wakeup Active Squelch (RWAS), which enhances its performance when operating with another RWAS compatible radio. In standby mode the radio will go into "sleep" mode to conserve the battery. Periodically the system will enter "sniff" modes and listen for a digital burst from another RWAS unit, to "wake it up." This unit is shown with the KY-99 Crypto device attached.

second signal called Standard Positioning Service (SPS) is available for civilian and commercial use.

The current GPS unit is the Rockwell "Plugger," or PSN-11. The precise name for the unit is, PLGR96 (Precise Lightweight GPS Receiver). The PLGR96 is the most advanced version of the U.S. Department of Defense hand-held GPS unit. It addressed the increasingly demanding requirements of the Force Recon, as well as all the U.S. Special Operations Forces.

In addition to the team being supplied with a PLGR, each member of the Force Recon will normally carry a personal GPS unit, such as the Garmin 12 or the newer eTrex models. These Commercial Off The Shelf (COTS) units provide the Marine with a user-friendly device capable of serving the needs of the team while also acting as a personal E&R (Escape and Recovery) device.

SIDS

Secondary Imagery Dissemination System or (SIDS) equipment and procedures are used in the electronic transmission and receipt of digital imagery and imagery products in other than real or near-real time. Secondary Image Dissemination is the process of post-collection electronic dissemination of Command, Control, Communications, and Intelligence (C3I) digital imagery and associated data, over a time interval ranging from near-real time to a period of days, at a level of quality determined by receiver requirements. The SIDS is used by the Force Reconnaissance Marines to transmit secondary images, facsimile messages, and so forth, in tactical and strategic environments.

U.S. Marine Corps Secondary Imagery Dissemination System (SIDS) collects, transmits, and receives, current and archived imagery electronically throughout the MAGTF using available communications paths. They support intelligence, weaponry, and targeting for air and ground forces. The system is composed of a Canon Digital Camera, day and night lenses/

AN/PRC-150 radio provides long-range capabilities for the Marines. The radio is capable of both encrypted voice and data communications, and can display and transmit precision location beamed by external GPS (Global Positioning System) receivers.

AN/PRC-148 (V) Maritime MultiBand Inter/Intra Team Radio (MBITR), called the "M-Biter" by the Force Recon Marines. This compact, hand-held individual tactical radio measures a scant 8.4 inches long x 2.6 inches wide x 1.5 inches deep. It is AM/FM, voice or data, VHF or UHF (continuous coverage from 30-512 MHz) and is waterproof to two atmospheres. Additionally, the MBITR has imbedded Crypto capability, and because of the beacon it can double as a Personal Survival radio. When attached to the AN/PSN-11 GPS (PLGR96) it allows digital transmission of the operator's location when the radio is keyed. Weighing in at a mere 2.7 pounds with batteries installed, the GPS unit is easily stowed in the cavernous rucksack or even in a pocket of an assault vest worn by the Force Recon Marines.

The Digital Communications Terminal or DCT is a hand-held communications device that can be operated with radios, field wire, and switchboards with its own accessory equipment. It is used to compose, edit, display, transmit, and receive message and map information. The DCT is a self-contained unit that can use an internal 9-volt battery or external power source. Here it is connected to a AN/PRC-138.

image intensifier, Lightweight Digital Image Processor, keyboard, modem, and Harris Universal Image Transmission Software or HUITS. Once the images are captured, the camera is connected to the computer and the images are then transmitted over comm equipment.

The addition of SIDS to the Force Recon T/O provides the team with the capability of providing real-time images, giving the MEU(SOC) commander a view of "eyes" on the target. Staff Sergeant Joe Tablada, 4th Force Recon, relates that during Exercise Pacific Rim, his team used the SIDS while they were doing a recon of a

target for a DA op. The team was able to present digitally to the assault force the actual layout of the target, and OPFOR personnel guarding the position. Equipped with these images, the GCE made the modifications needed to the assault plan and carried off the attack without a glitch.

AN/PVS-14 Night Vision Device

The AN/PVS-14D is the optimum night vision monocular ensemble for special applications. The monocular or pocket-scope can be hand held, mounted on a facemask or helmet, or attached to a weapon. The new PVS-14D night vision monocular offers the latest, state-of-the-art capability in a package that meets the rigorous demands of the U.S. Military's Special Operations Force. The monocular configuration is important to shooters who want to operate with night vision, while maintaining dark adaptation in the opposite eye. The head mount assembly, a standard in the kit, facilitates hands-free operation when helmet wear is not required. The weapon mount allows for use in a variety of applications, from using your iron sights to coupling with a red dot or tritium sighting system such as the Aimpoint Comp M/ML, Trijicon ACOG system. A compass is available to allow for the user to view the bearing in the night vision image.

Intra-Team communications is essential to a successful operation. Here, Capt. Andy Christian, Commander 6th Platoon, 2nd Force Recon Company, displays the headsets used by the Marines to maintain comm link between team members. The pliable rubber ear cup establishes contact with the operator's head, to lessen ambient sounds. The headset has an adjustable elastic strap allowing the user to comfortably wear the device whether Fast Roping, moving under fire, or even swimming. The unit is sealed to allow the team to insert via water.

AN/PEQ-1A SOFLAM

The AN/PEQ-1A Special Operations Forces - Laser Acquisition Marker (SOFLAM) is utilized in a direct action mission for the direction of terminal guided ordnance (TGO). This technique is referred to as "lasing the target." When a target absolutely, positively has to be destroyed, you put a team on the ground and a fast mover with a smart bomb in the air; results are one smoking bomb crater. This newly issued laser-marking device is lighter and more compact than the current laser marker in service with the U.S. military. It provides the operators with the capability to locate and designate critical enemy targets for destruction utilizing laser-guided ordinance. It can be utilized in daylight or, with the attached night vision optics, at night.

The SOFLAM, officially called the Ground Laser Target Designator (GLTD II) by the manufacturer, Northrop Grumman, is a compact, lightweight, portable laser target designator and rangefinder. The SOFLAM is capable of exporting range data via an RS422 link and importing azimuth and elevation. It was designed to enable special operations forces to direct laser-guided smart weapons, such as Paveway bombs, Hellfire missiles, and Copperhead munitions. The AN/PEQ-1A can be implemented as part of a sophisticated, digitized fire-control system with thermal or image-intensified sights.

The SIDS system is comprised of a Canon Digital Camera, day and night lenses/image intensifier, Lightweight Digital Image Processor, keyboard, and modem, and Harris Universal Image Transmission Software or HUITS. HIUTS is used for reconnaissance, surveillance, intelligence gathering and other applications that require the MEF(SOC) to see and evaluate real-time imagery and data.

Once the images are captured the camera is connected to the processor, and the images are then transmitted over the team's comm equipment. HUITS is a Microsoft-Windows NT/2000/XP-compatible software for high-speed and dependable transmission of high-resolution digital images, motion video clips, text, and other data over tactical radio communications channels.

AN/PVS-14 Night Vision Monocular may be hand-held, worn on a head mount assembly, mounted on the U.S. Military PAGST Kevlar combat helmet, or can be mounted directly on the operator's weapon. The mount incorporates adjustments front and back, and flip-up/flip-down capability. An optional three-power (3x) focal magnifier lens assembly is designed to temporarily attach to the objective lens for long-range viewing. One of the primary benefits of the PVS-14 is the fact that, since it covers only one eye, the operator will have "night vision" in one eye and ambient night sight in the other. It also can be fitted on the RAS of the M4A1. With the attachment of the NOD (Night Optical Device) to the weapon, it will accommodate precision-aimed firing. It can also be used in conjunction with the Aimpoint and ACOG 4x32 gunsight.

A Force Recon team with an AN/PEQ-1A SOFLAM. In a process known a "lasing" or "painting," the operator illuminates a target with a laser designator and then the munition, a smart bomb, guides to a spot of laser energy reflected from the target. The SOFLAM has the capability to range out to 20 kilometers and can designate to 5 kilometers. The unit weighs 12.6 pounds and has a 10x magnification. The unit is readily integrated with other Day/Night Observation Systems Range, Azimuth, Elevation, and BIT Displays.

The SOFLAM uses the PRF or Pulse Repetition Frequency that can be set to NATO STANAG Band I or II, or is programmable. (Note: STANAG represents Standards and Agreements set forth by NATO, for the process, procedures, terms, and conditions under which Mutual Government Quality Assurance of defense products are to be performed by the appropriate National Authority of one NATO member nation, at the request of another NATO member nation or NATO Organization.) PRF is the number of pulses per second transmitted by a laser.

Full Spectrum Battle Equipment (FSBE)

The FSBE was designed specifically for Maritime Special Purpose Force (MSPF) Amphibious Raids. The FSBE is an Amphibious Assault

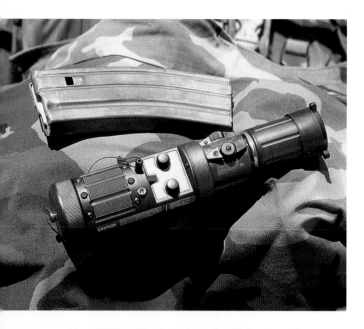

The AN/PEQ-4. Officially designated as Medium Power Laser Illuminator (MPLI), unofficially the Force Recon Marines refer to it as the "Light Saber." The PEQ-4 is a hand-held IR laser pointer, designed to illuminate and mark targets for night-vision-capable aircraft and supporting arms out to 10 kilometers. It is powered by six AA batteries and is waterproof to two atmospheres.

Seen here is the new issue MS-2000(M) Strobe light. This omnidirectional white light is equivalent to 250,000 lumens. It is also fitted with an IR (Infrared) shield visible only with NVGs and features a blue filter, which differentiates the signal of the strobe from ground fire. The MS-2000(M) replaces the older SDU-5, strobe. Don't leave the harbor site without one.

Vest (AAV), which will accept an assortment of load-bearing devices. Pockets, pouches, or a variety of tools, gear and gadgets can be attached to the vest. The AAV will also work in conjunction with the Small Arms Protective Insert (SAPI) to protect the Marines from small arms and fragments. It is fitted with a quick-release cutaway permitting the operator to drop the system directly off his body with one pull. The pull-ring may be tucked beneath the vest so it is readily available for the operator, yet will not get snagged on items in an operational environment.

Also part of the FSBE system is the LPU-34/P Recon Version Type II flotation collar which is attached to the vest. The vest provides up to 72 pounds of positive buoyancy and can be worn during the operation. The Modular Integrated Communications Helmet (MICH) accepts a wide assortment of radio devices for inter/intra team communications; additionally it provides the Marines with improved ballistic and impact protection.

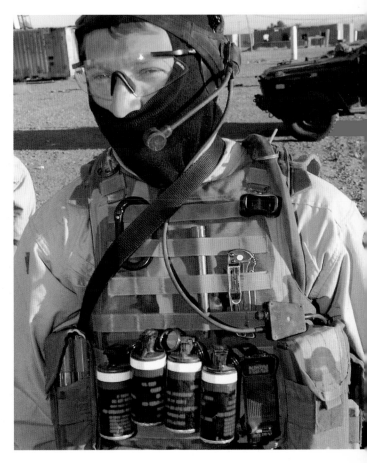

The Full Spectrum Battle Equipment (FSBE) ensemble integrates load-bearing and water-safety equipment with tactical body armor. The FSBE provides for decreased weight, flotation, emergency air, and mobility (easily removable, light weight, streamlined and modular body armor). Another feature of the FSBE is the quick release setup allowing the operator to jettison the FSBE in the event of an emergency.

Deployed with the 26th MEU(SOC) in Khandahar, Afghanistan, Staff Sgt Dan Bourdaghs of 3rd Platoon 2nd Force Recon Company is geared up and ready for action prior to a raid in support of Operation Enduring Freedom. Attached to his combat vest are "Flash-Bang" grenades, folding combat knife, chem-lights, ammunition magazines and other mission essential equipment. Next to the Chem-lights he is carrying a LPL-30Z , which is a lightweight, compact, hand-held IR long-range laser pointer/illuminator. It is designed to mark targets for both aircraft and ground units, Combat Search And Rescue, Air-Ground signaling, (i.e., Infil/Exfil activities), and a variety of other applications. The LPL-30 enables the Force Recon Marines to pinpoint and designate targets or other objects at distances up to 4 km (or 10 km using the LPL-30-SL/Z). *USMC Photo*

CHAPTER 7

Techniques

Fast Rope Insertion System (FRIS)

Fast Rope Insertion System is the preferred method of insertion when you need to get to the ground fast! This system begins with small woven ropes made of wool, which are then braided into a larger rope. The rope is rolled into a deployment bag and the end secured to the helicopter. Depending on the model of chopper, it can be just outside on the hoist mechanism of the side door or attached to a bracket off the back ramp. Once over the insertion point, the rope is deployed, and even as it is hitting the ground the ODA members are jumping onto the woolen line and sliding down as easily as a fireman goes down a pole. Once the team is safely on the ground the flight engineer or gunner—depending on the type of helicopter—will pull the safety pin, and the rope will fall to the ground. Such a system is extremely useful in the rapid deployment of Force Recon personnel: an entire assault team can be inserted within 10 to 15 seconds. FRIS is the most accepted way of getting a force onto the ground expeditiously. Unlike rappelling, once the trooper hits the ground, he is "free" of the rope and can begin his mission. ·

The Special Patrol, Insertion & Extraction System (SPIES)

While fast roping gets you down quick, there are times when you have to extract just as fast. The problem is, there is no LZ for the helicopter to land, and the "bad guys" are closing in on your position. Marine Corps riggers developed the Special Patrol, Insertion & Extraction System (SPIES) during the Vietnam War. It is similar in concept to the Army Special Forces-designed McGuire or STABO rig. A single rope is lowered from the hovering helicopter. Attached to this rope are rings, woven and secured into the rope at approximately five-feet intervals. There can be as many as eight rings on the rope. The team members, wearing special harnesses similar to a parachute harness, will attach themselves to the rope, via the rings. This is accomplished by clipping in a snap link that is at the top of the harness.

Once all team members are secured, a signal is given and the Recon team is extracted out of harm's way. This method allows the team to maintain covering fire from their weapons as they extract. Once the team has been whisked out of enemy range, and a LZ can be located, the helicopter pilot will bring the troops to ground again. At this time they will disconnect from the rope and board the chopper, which will then complete the extraction.

HALO/HAHO

There are times when, for political, strategic, or tactical considerations, a team cannot just drop into an enemy's backyard. You must insert your team clandestinely from afar and outside of the nation's territorial airspace or boundaries. For such an insertion, the Force Recon Marines would use either High Altitude Low Opening (HALO) or High Altitude High Opening (HAHO).

These type of parachute operations will be flights over or adjacent to the objective area from altitudes not normally associated with conventional static-line parachuting. HALO/HAHO infiltrations are normally conducted under the

FRIS, Fast Rope Insertion System, is the express elevator to the battlefield. By employing the FRIS, the Force Recon team can be inserted in a matter of seconds. Unlike rappelling, once the trooper hits the ground, he is "free" of the rope and can begin his mission. Here a team of Force Recon Marines Fast Ropes from a CH-53 onto a rooftop during a TRUEX in Dayton, Ohio.

While everyone is focused on Fast Roping, the Marines of Force Recon still maintain training in the skill of rappelling. There are times when you have to abseil down the side of a mountain, bridge, or building and this calls for rope work, not an aerial platform. The limitations of rappelling are that the Marine is connected to the rope via carabineer, which he must disconnect upon reaching the ground. Nevertheless, when inserting a team with heavy rucksacks for a Deep Recon mission, rappelling can be a viable option.

cover of darkness or at twilight to lessen the chance of observation by hostile forces. Using the Ram Air Parachute System (RAPS), operators deploy their parachutes at a designated altitude, assemble in the air, and land together in the arranged drop zone (DZ) to begin their mission. This type of drop can be conducted even in adverse weather conditions.

Flying at an altitude of 25,000 to 43,000 feet MSL (mean sea level), the jump aircraft, such as a Combat Talon, will appear as legitimate aircraft on an enemy's radar screen—perhaps just another commercial airliner traversing the globe. What the radar operator will not know is that the aircraft is the launching platform for the world's most lethal weapon system: a team of highly trained Force Recon Marines.

Military Free-Fall operations are ideally adapted for the infiltration of Force Recon teams. While the maximum exit altitude is 43,000 feet MSL, Military Free-Fall (MFF) operations may be as low as 5,000 feet above ground level (AGL). A typical team can be deployed in a fraction of the time it would take a conventional static-line jump. Normal opening altitudes range from 3,500 AGL to 25,000 MSL dependent on mission parameters.

Military Free-Fall (MFF) parachuting enables the MFF commander to infiltrate a recon team into areas where it would be impossible to conduct static-line parachute operations. The Deep Reconnaissance missions of Force Recon often require rapid and covert infiltrations into operational areas.

As the aircraft approaches the insertion point, the ramp will lower. The combination of aircraft noise and wearing the MFF parachutist helmet and an oxygen mask makes any normal verbal communication almost impossible. For this reason, the team will communicate with the use of arm-and-hand signals or radios. Having already received the signals to don helmets, unfasten seat belts, and check oxygen, the jumpmaster waits for the team to signal back "OK."

Approximately two minutes before the insertion, the jumpmaster raises his arm upward from his side indicating the team should stand up. Next he extends his arm straight out at shoulder level, palm up, then bends it to touch his helmet, this indicating move to the rear. The insertion team, equipped with ram-air parachutes, oxygen masks, and goggles, stand up and get ready to jump. If jumping from the side jump door, the lead man will station himself a meter away from the door; if going out the rear of the plane, the lead man will stop at the hinge of the cargo ramp. With their rucksacks or combat assault vests loaded with mission-essential equipment, they head toward the rear of the plane. Moments turn into an eternity and then it is time. As the aircraft reaches the proper coordinates for the drop, the jump light emits a steady green. The command is given, "Go!" In a matter of seconds the team heads down the ramp and out into the darkness as the drone of the plane's engines fades off in the distance.

Depending on the mission parameters, they will perform a HALO or HAHO jump. In HALO, the team will exit the plan and Free-Fall through the airspace, meeting up at a prearranged time or altitude. Jumping in this manner, the team is so small that they are virtually invisible to the naked eye, and of course will not show up on any enemy radar screen. Using GPS units and altimeters, the

The Special Patrol Insertion Extraction System is used for getting "outta Dodge" in a hurry. It consists of a synthetic-fiber, eight-strand braid, 1 3/4 inches in diameter. The tensile strength of the rope is 35,000 pounds, the ring at the top of the sleeve at 2,500 pounds, and the sleeve at 9,000 pounds. SPIES comes in lengths of 60 feet, 90 feet, and 120 feet. There is a 3/16-inch steel-cable safety line rated at 3,700 pounds, as well as a steel-locking snaplink with a strength of 5,500 pounds.
Defense Visual Information Center

team will descend until fairly close to the drop zone. At that point they will open their chutes and prepare for the very short trip to the ground.

The alternate method, HAHO, is also jumping from an extreme height with oxygen. The difference from HALO is that as soon as the team jumps off, they immediately deploy their parachutes and use them to glide into a denied area. For this type of jump, they would also utilize GPS units and altimeters. In order to maintain

HALO/HAHO is a prime method of inserting a Force Recon team into enemy territory. Due to extreme cold encountered during high-altitude parachute operations at 25,000 feet and above, the jumpers must have adequate protection in this environment. This Force Recon Marine is suited up in the Parachutist Individual Equipment Kit (PIEK), a complete ensemble consisting of individual parachutist clothing and equipment to meet the demands of high altitude Military Free-Fall (MFF) and static line MC-5 parachute operations. This includes a Gore-tex Jumpsuit, Polartec Jumpsuit Liner, Cotton Ripstop Jumpsuit, Aviator's Gloves, Gore-tex Cold-weather Gloves, Overboots, and MA2-30 altimeter. The standard parachutist helmet is the HGU-55/P. The jumper may utilize the snap-down visor or wear goggles to protect his eyes during free-fall descent. The mask attached to the helmet is the MBU-12P pressure demand oxygen mask used for high altitude operations. Additionally, the helmet is equipped with a communication system to allow team members to talk with each other.

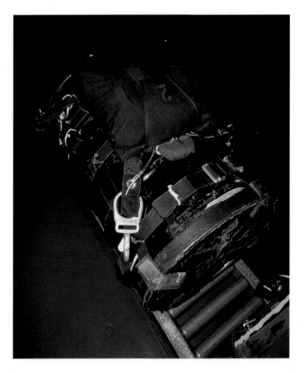

Tandem Offset Resupply Delivery System (TORDS) comprises a 55-gallon drum filled with ammunition, food, comm gear, and other equipment. It is attached to a jumper, and as the name implies, they exit the aircraft "in-tandem". This method is also useful if you need to insert mission-essential personnel who are not jump qualified. Additionally there are larger containers up to seven feet tall, which can be used to deliver up to 650 to 950 pounds of equipment.

formation integrity, each jumper would have a strobe on his helmet, either normal or IR, and the team would wear the appropriate NVGs. Additionally, each man in the team would communicate via radio for command and control of the insertion, as well as formation on the DZ.

There are a number of advantages of utilizing the HALO/HAHO procedures. There are times when, due to the presence of enemy air defenses, it is the best means to infiltrate a team into a hostile area; this also increases the survivability of the support aircraft. If the mission requires the team to jump into a mountainous terrain were it would not be practical or prudent to attempt a static-line parachute operation, MFF would be a practical option. Other benefits include times when navigational aids (NAVAIDS) are not available to guarantee the requisite precision of drops at low altitudes, such as deserts or jungle environments. MFF is used when necessary to land the team at multiple points of an objective for the purpose of attacking or seizing a primary target and when success requires a low-signature infiltration.

MC-5 Static Line/Free-Fall Ram Air Parachute System (SL/FF RAPS)

The MC-5 RAPS is the primary parachute for inserting Force Reconnaissance Marines for deep reconnaissance or other DA missions. The MC-5 SL/FF RAPS can be configured for static line or Free-Fall, depending on mission requirements. The MC-5 integrates components of the Paraflite MT-1XX Interim RAPS, the MC-4 RAPS, and the MT-1XS S/L convertible static line system into one versatile parachute system. The system uses identical main and reserve canopies, which not only reduce the logistics involved with separate canopies, but also eliminate the training, maintenance, and operational use of a different size and configuration of reserve canopy.

The system's identical main and reserve parachutes, which can be interchanged, are 370

Deep behind enemy lines noise is kept to a bare minimum, with the team relying on hand signals to communicate. Here, the point man uses the hand signal to communicate to the team to "Freeze!" This signal is passed down along the line from Marine to Marine.

square feet, seven-celled, and manufactured from 1.1-ounce F-111 nylon ripstop fabric. A cotton reinforcement and buffering panel is installed on the top and bottom skin of the canopy. The deployment sequence for the reserve canopy incorporates a free-bag system, which consists of a spring-loaded pilot chute, a bridle, and a deployment bag. The harness and container

A term carried over from Force Recon operations in Vietnam and still applied to today's rear guard is "Tail End Charlie." His responsibility, as the name implies, is to bring up the rear, providing protection for the team. In the event the team makes contact and must reverse their direction, he will become the "pointman" to get the team out of harm's way, ASAP!

assembly has a two-pin main container to accommodate the static line. The leg straps/chest strap are fitted with quick ejector snaps.

Tandem Offset Resupply Delivery System (TORDS)

TORDS provides Force Reconnaissance companies with a parachute delivery system that can supply or resupply reconnaissance teams with combat-essential equipment or personnel. This system has a payload capacity in excess of 500 pounds. The TORDS has a square main and reserve canopy. The canopies are manufactured from 1.1 ounce F-111 ripstop nylon fabric. The deployable system for the reserve canopy incorporates a free-bag system, which consists of a spring-loaded pilot chute, a bridle, and a deployable bag. The reserve free-bag is not connected to the canopy and will be jettisoned during deployment. The TORDS has a six-foot drogue parachute, which is deployed to reduce the terminal velocity of the tandem master and load (passenger/combat equipment) to approximately 120 miles per hour upon reaching opening altitude. A ripcord is pulled to release the drogue, which then acts as a pilot chute and deploys the main canopy. The TORDS comes complete with a passenger harness and a combat equipment container.

Sergeant William J "Plug" Daniels, 2nd Force Recon Jumpmaster, explains:

The Tandem Offset Resupply Delivery System (TORDS) was adopted for use by the Marine Corps around 1997. Experienced Military Free-fall parachutists, minimum of 200 jumps, and MFF jumpmasters were chosen for the program. The system was adopted to give Free-fall teams the ability to take non-jump-qualified personnel in on a specified mission, or to jump and land together with large, heavy loads of equipment. The max-all-up weight for the MC-5 is 360 pounds; with the TORDS all up can be 650 pounds for training or 950 pounds for combat situations. When jumping a passenger, the pair will exit the aircraft with all of their equipment on them, rucksacks, weapons, and oxygen and land with all of it. When jumping equipment we found the largest container that should be

A Harbor Site, also referred to as a Patrol Base, is a relatively secure operational site where forward-deployed reconnaissance elements may operate communications/electronics equipment or rest during advance force or special missions. Typically, this is an area located in thick vegetation where the team will take refuge for the night. The position ideally will be in an out-of-the-way location, which will provide cover and concealment for the team. Additionally, the team will look for a spot that is virtually inaccessible so any enemy force approaching their position will draw attention to themselves, thus alerting the team, whereupon they can prepare to engage or egress from the site. Here, Sgt. Steven Little of 5th Platoon, 2nd Force Recon mans the radio at the team's Harbor Site.

A "Tight 360" is used during an extended halt of the team. The team forms in a 360° perimeter, with each member of the team observing his sector of responsibility. Here, members of 6th Platoon, 2nd Force Reconnaissance Company demonstrate a "Tight 360." Each member of the six-man team will cover his sector providing security for the team. Shown here in the open for demonstration purposes, the team would normally seek a location which would afford them proper cover and concealment.

Off all the techniques and procedures employed by Force Recon, the most indispensable is the ability to disappear into their environment. This can be seen in this picture, where a recon team has "gone to ground." Stealth, cover, and concealment are the indispensable skills of a Force Recon Marine.

Here they are! The Recon team stands to reveal its position.

jumped is three feet in diameter by seven feet tall because of aerodynamics. The best thing about tandem, with equipment rather than airdrop that is the tandem master is in control and lands with the equipment whereas airdropped equipment would land away from the team and they would have to find it and recover it, increasing the time spent linking up and moving out.

You load the equipment on the aircraft and put it on rollers. The tandem master hooks up to it about six minutes out. The tandem master is wearing a small parachute on his front, hooked up to all the points you would hook the passenger to. Coming off of that parachute container is a ten-foot tether that the bundle is hooked to. When you exit you push the bundle on the rollers until it leaves the ramp and let go of it and you dive out after it. When we jump equipment we use a drogue setter. He sets the

drogue for you as you leave the ramp. We use a 72-inch drogue for equipment so it will slow the jumper down to normal free-fall velocity (about 120 miles per hour). So until he gets to pull altitude he has the drogue above him. He is in the middle and the equipment is 10 feet below him. When he gets to pull altitude and releases the drogue, it acts as the pilot chute to deploy the main. Unless something goes wrong, he lands with the equipment attached. If he has to cut the main chute away, there is a release handle he can pull to release the bundle, and it will come down under a parachute.

LAR-V Re-breather

LAR stands for Lung Automatic Re-breather. It is a closed-circuit system, meaning it does not give off any telltale bubbles to compromise the swimmer. The LAR-V MK 25 provides a Force Recon combat diver with enough oxygen to stay under the water for up to four hours. The exact time will depend on the individual diver's rate of breathing and his depth in the water.

Oxygen Flow
LAR-V Re-breather

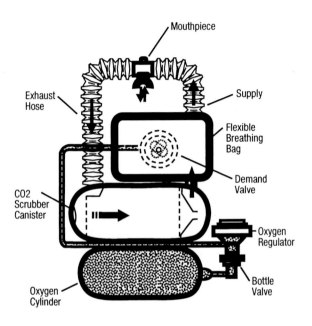

Mouthpiece

Exhaust Hose

Supply

Flexible Breathing Bag

Demand Valve

CO2 Scrubber Canister

Oxygen Regulator

Oxygen Cylinder

Bottle Valve

The closed-circuit oxygen UBA currently in service with Force Recon is the Draegar LAR-V MK 25. The closed-circuit system prevents any exhaust bubbles from being seen on the surface of the water, thus making it easier for the team to infiltrate to their objective without being observed by enemy forces. This Marine is also wearing the SECUMAR TSK 2/42 life preserver, which serves as a buoyancy device, rescue unit, and lifejacket. On each side of the preserver are holders for compressed air cylinders.

Closed-circuit oxygen re-breather is a specialized type of underwater breathing apparatus (UBA) in which all exhaled gas is kept within the rig. As it is exhaled, the gas is carried via the exhalation hose to an absorbent canister through a carbon dioxide-absorbent bed that removes the carbon dioxide by chemically reacting with the carbon dioxide produced as the diver breathes. After the unused oxygen passes through the canister, the gas travels to the breathing bag where it is available to be inhaled again by the diver.

The gas supply used in the LAR-V is pure oxygen, which prevents inert gas buildup in the diver and allows all the gas carried by the diver to be used for metabolic needs. Closed–circuit oxygen UBA offers advantages valuable to Force Recon, including stealth infiltration, extended operating duration, and less weight than open-circuit SCUBA.

Combat Rubber Reconnaissance Craft (CRRC)

The CRRC or F-470 Zodiac is utilized by the Force Recon teams for insertion to perform various reconnaissance missions and assorted waterborne operations. This small, lightweight, inflatable, rugged raft has replaced the IBS or Inflatable Boat, Small. With operational configurations 265 pounds and 15.5 feet in length and 6.3 feet wide the CRRC is capable of being deployed from both the CH-53 and CH-46; albeit when stuffed into the Sea Knight you must remove some of the air and scrunch it together a little.

To power the CRRC, the Marines use the Improved Military Amphibious Reconnaissance System (I-MARS) 35-horsepower engine. The I-MARS outboard is a combination of the 35-horsepower Military Amphibious Reconnaissance System (MARS) outboard motor and a pump jet. The pump jet takes the place of the propeller in order to provide the user with a safer outboard motor. The I-MARS gives the Marine Corps the capability to insert and extract personnel from the shore with the CRRC more safely, and without degrading the overall performance of the old MARS outboard motor or CRRC. The I-MARS can be operated in any environment in which the MARS outboard motor previously has been used. Currently under testing is the new

The reconnaissance mission of a United States Marine brings him to hostile areas throughout the world—areas where he is expected to infiltrate and exfiltrate undetected, recurrently, to conduct reconnaissance or other combat action missions. Often the Reconnaissance Marine must enter his objective area underwater in order to achieve a clandestine approach and increase the chances for mission success. Note that the green tubing and webbing in use is the "buddy line." Each of the team members is attached via the webbing, keeping the team together as they swim.

55-horsepower engine to give the Marines more power and speed to get out of harm's way as quickly as they get in.

Interim Fast Attack Vehicles (IFAV)

The Marine Corp's Interim Fast Attack Vehicle (IFAV) is a Daimler Chrysler model of the Mercedes-Benz MB 290 GD 1.5-ton truck off-road vehicle built as the Wolf Gelaendegaengige Kleinfahrzeuge (small all-terrain vehicle) for the German Bundeswehr. First deployed to a U.S. Marine unit in November 1999, the IFAV replaces its early 1980s counterpart, the M-151 Fast Attack Vehicle, which previously served as a smaller attack version of the Humvee. Of major importance to Marine commanders is the increased

The Zodiac F-470 Combat Rubber Raiding Craft or CRRC is one of the primary methods of insertion for the Force Recon Marines. Here, members of 1st Platoon, 4th Force Recon Company practice a beach insertion in Kaneohe Bay, Hawaii. Each member of the team is on alert, with the SAW gunner poised on the bow of the raft ready to suppress any hostile fire as they approach the shoreline.

Two Force Recon Marines HELO-cast from the rear cargo ramp of a CH-46 Sea Knight. The helicopter pilot must maintain a hover approximately 10 to 12 feet off the surface, often a tricky position as there is no point of reference but the undulating waves beneath the aircraft.

offensive power the IFAV offers. A primary advantage of the IFAV is its ability to be transported internally by Marine Corps workhorse aircraft, including the CH-46 Sea Knight, CH-53 Sea Stallion, and in the future, the V-22 Osprey. Additionally, it can be parachute dropped behind enemy lines by aircraft taking off from forward deployed Navy ships. Other improvements to the IFAV have made it far superior to the M-151 in most respects. The M-151 didn't quite have

the mobility, speed, or durability to get Marines into the environments they will need to be in during the 21st century. Run by safer diesel fuel and equipped with greater handling ability, the IFAV appears to be tailor-made for the Marine Corps. Members of 2nd Platoon, 1st Force Recon Company, utilized the IFAV for mobile reconnaissance, raids, and interdiction in southern Afghanistan in support of Operation Enduring Freedom.

Force Recon is currently using the IFAV to perform long-range deep penetration recon missions. Seen here in use with 1st Force Recon Company in Afghanistan. The normal crew is team leader, driver, gunner, and assistant gunner. The vehicle will take a wide assortment of weapons including the M240G, Mk19 40mm grenade cannon, and M2 .50-caliber machine gun. Weighing in at 7760 pounds with an overall length of 180 inches and width of 63.5 inches it is currently the only vehicle capable of being transported in the MV-22 Osprey. The compact military SUV has a range well over 300 miles; a maximum road speed of 96 mph; with an estimated fuel consumption of 18 mpg. It can ford water to a depth of 30 inches making it suitable for Marine Corps operations. *Photo Courtesy ForceRecon.org*

CHAPTER 8 *Force Recon Into the Future*

The future of Marine Force Reconnaissance is integrated in the future of the U.S. Marine Corps; in order to look at the bearing towards which Force Recon is heading, we must explore the course that the USMC is proceeding upon. In a message to the Marines on 12 September 2001, the Commandant of the Marine Corps, General James L. Jones, Jr., related, "The recent terrorist attacks on our nation highlight the new reality of warfare. . . . Our focus on developing Anti-terrorism and Force Protection (AT/FP) capabilities across our force continues our tradition of innovation and transformation. . . . While our expeditionary culture remains the centerpiece of our warfighting capability, the added ability to effectively deal with terrorism is critical today and will remain one of our core capabilities for the foreseeable future. . . . Our expeditionary culture has once again proven valuable to our nation and we are poised to respond. . . . In conjunction with the Navy, we have once again demonstrated the value of the Navy-Marine Corps team in responding across the full spectrum of capabilities that our nation demands."

After the deployments of the MEU(SOC) forces into the Afghanistan theater of operations in support of America's War on Terrorism, General Jones reaffirmed this resolve a year later. Addressing a group of Marines on a TRUEX in Dayton, Ohio, he conveyed to them, "The MEUs have performed outstanding during their involvement in Operation Enduring Freedom. Such operations create an aperture to the importance of the MEFs."

From the new "Pixel" camouflage uniforms to the MV-22 "Osprey," the Marines are updating their forces. Future developments in the Marine Expeditionary Warfare will see the introduction of more modern naval platforms from which the Marines will be launched. The Navy's newest class of ship, *San Antonio* (LPD 17), is scheduled to replace the older LPD 4 class, and its increased vehicle- and substantial cargo-carrying capacity will make it a key element of 21 century Amphibious Ready Groups. Additionally, the High Speed Vessel or HSV will bring the Marines on-site faster than any previous ship. Forthcoming strategies may see the Amphibious Ready Groups evolve into Amphibious Strike Groups by augmenting the current ARG with a Carrier Battle Group. Such an armada would be more than capable of projecting a force from the sea. In fact, in many countries of the world, an invading ASG would grossly outnumber their standing armies.

Pushing the envelope even further in the area of Total Force Projection from the sea is the strategic plan for deploying Marines from Sea Based Platforms. These platforms or network of platforms would be similar to current oil platforms in use today; however, they would be larger, more seaworthy, and movable. Sea Basing will permit Marine forces to initiate sustainable operations, as well as facilitate the flow of follow-on forces into the theater. Such a mobile platform would allow the Marines to provide a base of operation well off of any hostile shore, in international waters. No longer would the United States have to gain permission to establish a landing base or airfield for our forces. This secure, self-sustaining island of power would bring "gunboat diplomacy" to a whole new dimension.

Since their creation in 1775, the U.S. Marine Corps has stood ready and capable as America's premier Total Force In Readiness, promoting peace, stability, and the ability to defeat any foe anytime, anywhere, anyplace. As the Marines forge ahead into the 21 century and the new wave of warfare confronting them, the Marines of Force Recon will serve as the eyes on the target and the boots on the ground.

This Marine is armed with an M4A1, Aimpoint sight, AN/PEQ-2, MBITR with headset, strobe, MUS(SOC) .45-cal. sidearm, and other mission-essential gear. The latest weaponry, optics, laser sights, and communications equipment are powerful tools in the hands of a highly trained, mature, and proficient operator who has the tenacity and aggressiveness of a U.S. Marine. All this, combined with the support of the MEU(SOC), make the Force Recon Marine undeniably the "ultimate smart weapon!"

While the above constitutes a strategic course of action for the Marines, there is the need to address the tactical environment and equipment required to achieve these strategies. For this purpose, the Force Recon Marines turn to the Marine Corps Systems Command, Raids and Recon unit at Quantico, Virginia. The mission of the MCSC is to serve as the Commandant's primary agent for equipping the Operating Forces, allowing them to accomplish their warfighting missions. MCSC is the recognized leader in equipping the Marines to be victorious in combat. They continually seek the improvement of systems and equipment for the operations forces and will manage the systems and equipment during their entire life cycle.

MCSC is responsible for a wide assortment of activities, from simple armament improvements such as modifying the MEU(SOC) 45 pistol to accept a light or laser-aiming module, evaluating new equipment such as the Swimmer Propulsion unit or the Zodiac Armorflat, developing new insertion methods, and vehicles programs such as the IFAV. For example; Major Bob McCarthy, Deputy Project Manager for Raids and Recon, MCSC, relates, "Raids and Recon assisted in the Military Free-Fall Parachute Operational Evaluation of the MV-22."

Whether deployed from the ASG or a futuristic sea-based platform, a Zodiac or an MV-22, the Marines of Force Recon will function as an essential member of the MEF. They will continue to serve as the eyes and ears of the MEU(SOC) commander as they perform deep reconnaissance missions behind enemy lines. Their precision shooting and patrolling skills, along with their assault tactics will be indispensable in both Green Side and Black Side operations of any future conflicts. The Force Recon Marine is well placed in the community of excellence with the Corps.

Officially designated as Marine Corps Combat Utility Uniform, this new issue has what is often referred to as "Pixel" or "digital" camouflage. The new uniforms have rearranged pockets; the lower cargo pockets have been eliminated, the breast pockets slanted, and shoulder pockets added. Since full-battle gear—a flak jacket, load bearing vest, or FSBE—covers the front pockets, the shoulder pockets facilitate access to mission-essential items. The combat utility uniform comes with an embroidered Marine Corps eagle, globe, and anchor on the left breast pocket, eliminating the need for iron-on decals. The emblem is centered on the slanted pocket and parallel to the deck. The emblem is also reproduced in the material as a "watermark." Elastic has been added to the cargo pocket openings to ensure items are secured even if the pocket flap is not buttoned. This provides quick access without the concern of losing items as Marines engage targets from the prone position or as they assault their objective. There is no more mistaking Marines for SEALs; these unique uniforms are for the Corps only!

MV-22 Osprey is a tilt-rotor, vertical-takeoff-and-landing (VTOL) aircraft, which means it takes off like a helicopter and flies like a conventional airplane. The Osprey is a multi-engine, dual-piloted, self-deployable, medium-lift aircraft designed for combat, combat support, combat service support, and special missions. The MV-22 is planned as the placement for the Corps' aging squadrons of CH-46E and CH-53D medium-lift helicopters.

Manufactured by Zodiac of North America, the Armorflate is the first inflatable CRRC with an integrated bulletproof system. The Armorflate is a ballistic protection system comprised of a series of inflatable tubes to protect the troops from gunfire. The bulletproof material is provided by Simula, and is offered in both soft-and hard-armor protection. The system, which can be deployed in less than a minute, is shown here installed on the F-470 CRRC. Such systems as this are evaluated by the Marine Corps System Command to enhance the capabilities of the men going into battle. *Zodiac of North America*

Whether fighting in the desert, the jungles, or arctic regions, the Marines of Force Recon carry on in the proud heritage of those Recon Marines who have gone before. President Ronald Reagan commented on the U.S. Marines, "Some people go through their lives wondering if they made a difference in the world. The Marines do not have to ask this."

One of the most dynamic changes affecting Force Recon as the Marines head into the 21 century is the formation of a specialized Marine unit to be assigned to SOCOM. As mentioned earlier, the Marines were not part of the original SOCOM units on a SOF level. In January 2002, the Commandant presented the first official plans outlining the permanent force contribution the Marines could bring to SOCOM. In the course of developing this concept, three potential courses of actions materialized. First, the Marines would support SOCOM with their unique capabilities of forward-deployed MAGTFs. These MAGTFs would augment and sustain SOF capabilities. Second, Marine Units would be OPCON (Operational Command) to SOCOM on a recurring or rotational basis to execute designated missions. Third, the Corps would provide Marine forces to be permanently assigned to SOCOM as part of a Marine Special Operations Component or MARSOC.

As of this writing, MARSOC is in the development stages, with approximately a half-dozen scenarios and T/Os being evaluated. These plans range from rotational assignments of Force Recon assets under SOCOM, to the creation of an entirely new unit designed specially for SOF-type missions, with the unit mirroring the MSPF T/O. Command issues must also be resolved; will these Marines come under the Naval Special Warfare Command (NAVSPECWARCOM), or will they be a separate entity unto themselves?

The Force Reconnaissance Marines are more than capable of filling this niche within the SOF community. Whether in Green Side or Black Side

The Marine Corps Strategy 21 builds on core values, competencies, and signature characteristics of the Corps. Within this vision, the Marines remain America's Premier Expeditionary Total Force in Readiness, capable of a multitude of missions across a wide assortment of conflicts. The MAGTF concept is flexible to meet the combatant commanders' requirements, enable joint, allied, and coalition operation, and perform any other duties as directed by the Commander-In-Chief.

As the Marines of Force Recon embark on their missions, they not only bring with them the latest equipment, tactics, and techniques, they carry with them a set of values that has been fundamental to the Corps for over 200 years. Whether they will fast rope into a terrorist compound, or HELO into an embassy for a NEO, each of these warriors will also carry with him the courage, honor, and commitment of a United States Marine.

A pair of Marines from 2nd Force Reconnaissance Company prepare to move out on their next mission. It may be a Deep Recon to provide the MEU(SOC) with vital intel or to carry out a DA against a terrorist training camp. Whatever the mission, whenever the call, the Marines of Force Recon stand ready to answer, defend, and prevail.

operations, they will augment or compliment any current special operations team regardless of service. So exact are they in their tasks, Tier One assets aboard the *USS Kitty Hawk* during Operation Enduring Freedom reportedly requested Marine Force Recon teams to conduct their pre-assault reconnaissance.

Regarding the "elite" status of the Force Recon Marine, GySgt Ed Lynch, 6th Platoon, 2nd Force Reconnaissance Company, explains it best; "The Marine Corps is an elite organization within itself. Force Recon is a hand-picked unit that attains special skills. We are not special Marines; we are Marines who perform special tasks. It appears that the Marine Corps will soon join SOCOM and/ or JSOC in some capacity; regardless of that fact, no one Marine or group of Marines is more important than another. We are Marines first."

As the Marines maneuver further into the new millennium, the defense of our nation, our freedom, and our way of life will have a high priority. As our military rises to answer this call they will do so with new technology and sense of purpose. It is an interesting observation though, when you look at the recruiting campaigns of the various services: the Army offers education; the Navy, an adventure; the Air Force, technology. Yet the Marines still hold fast to the premise, "Every Marine is firstly a rifleman." Their recruitment emphasizes Honor, Courage, Commitment, and Country. As the U.S. military forces head off again to distant shores to defend America's interests, our dreams and freedom, the United States Marines will be on station. They will remain our Total Force In Readiness, and the men of Force Recon will provide them with the weapons to strike at the heart of any foe that would pose a threat to the United States of America. Semper Fi Marines!

Without a doubt the Marines of Force Recon are a special breed of men, their operations placing them at the tip of the spear. Melded with them are those who have gone before and infused in the Corps a heritage of valor as timeless as the seas from which they project their warfare, on missions from the islands of the Pacific in World War II to the wastelands of Afghanistan and beyond. While they do have a special mission, they are and remain . . . The Few . . . The Proud . . . The MARINES.

Terminology (Marine Talk)

Aft: The stern (rear) of a vessel, or toward that direction.

All hands: All members of a command.

As you were: Resume activity.

Astern: To the rear or behind you.

Aye, Aye, Sir: Correct form to acknowledge a direct order. Naval custom.

Bivouac: Term for a camp area in the field.

Boot: A Marine recruit.

Bow: The front portion of a ship.

Bridge: The portion of a ship's structure from which it is controlled.

Bulkhead: A wall.

C-4: Plastic explosive

Carry On: The order to resume previous activity.

Claymore: Anti-personnel mine, 700 steel balls packed in C-4.

Cobra: Helicopter gunship.

Corpsman or Doc: A Marine or Naval term for "medic."

Cover: Any form of headgear other than a helmet.

Det cord: Detonating cord, thin flexible plastic tube packed with explosive (PETN). Exploding at 25,000 fps.

DZ: Drop Zone.

FAC: Forward Air Controller.

Fast Movers: Marine, Navy, or Air Force jet fighters or fighter/bombers.

Field Day: Thorough cleaning of a room or area.

Fighting Hole: A position dug in the ground to provide cover and concealment, not same as Fox Hole.

Fire Team: The second smallest tactical unit in the Corps. The smallest is the individual rifleman. Three Marine riflemen and a Fire Team Leader make up a fire team.

FMF: Fleet Marine Force.

Galley: Shipboard kitchen; kitchen of a mess hall; mobile field kitchen.

Grunt: A Marine infantryman.

Gung-Ho: Chinese term for "working together." Understood as the team spirit.

Hatch: Door or doorway.

Hootch: Anything from a tent to a wooden hut.

Huey: Slang for UH-1 Helicopter, used for troop or cargo transport.

Junk on the Bunk: During inspection, a Marine lays out gear and uniforms on a flat surface, such as a bunk.

Ka-Bar: Marine's fighting knife.

Klick: Military slang for a kilometer, 1,000 meters or .62 of a mile.

LZ: Landing Zone.

MOS: Military Occupational Specialty, a Marine's primary training, e.g., 0300 (infantry), 0200 (intelligence), etc.

MRE: "Meal, Ready to Eat." Lightweight plastic packets of dehydrated food.

Mustang: An enlisted Marine who has obtained an Officer commission.

NCOIC: Non-Commissioned Officer In Charge.

Point or "point man": The Marine at the head of a patrol, the first guy in line.

Port: Left.

Rack: A bed.

Report: Presenting yourself or a group for which you are responsible to a superior.

Round: Bullet for a rifle or pistol or single load for any projectile-firing weapon.

Secure: To complete or end work on a project or the day's work.

SitRep: Situation Report.

Squared Away: Someone or something that makes a good impression. Well-maintained uniform or a successful exercise.

Starboard: Right.

Stow: Put away.

Topside: Upstairs.

782 Gear: The equipment a Marine carries in the field, including ALICE pace, web belt, suspenders, ammunition pouches, canteens, etc. Also called Deuce-gear.

Acronyms and Abbreviations

CAS	Close air support
CHOP	Change of operational control
CSAR	Combat search and rescue
CQB	Close quarters battle
DA	Direct action
DOD	Department of Defense
DZ	Drop zone
E&E	Evasion and escape
FEBA	Forward edge battle area
FOB	Forward operation base
FOL	Forward operating location
FRIES	Fast rope insertion / extraction system
FSCL	Fire support coordination line
GPS	Global positioning system
HAHO	High altitude high opening
HAMO	High altitude medium opening
HALO	High altitude low opening
HE	High explosive
HRST	Helicopter rope suspension training
HET	Human intelligence exploitation team
HUMINT	Human intelligence
INTREP	Intelligence report
IFAV	Interim fast attack vehicle
JCS	Joint Chiefs of Staff
LOS	Line of sight
LZ	Landing zone
MARFORLANT	Marine Forces Atlantic
MARFORPAC	Marine Forces Pacific
MARFORRES	Marine Forces Reserve
MOS	Military occupational specialty
MRE	Meal, ready to eat
NEC	Navy Enlisted Code (Navy version of MOS)
NOD	Night optical device
NVG	Night vision goggles
OPCON/M	Operational Control/Command
OPSEC	Operational security
PTP	Pre-deployment training program
ROC	Reconnaissance operating center
RECON	Reconnaissance
SEAL	Sea Air Land (U.S. Navy Special Operations Forces)
SAR	Search and rescue
SARC	Special amphibious reconnaissance corpsman
SF	Special Forces (U.S. Army)
SOF	Special operations forces
SOFLAM	Special operations forces–laser acquisition marker
SOCEX	Special operations capable exercise
SPIES	Special procedure infiltration/extraction system
STX	Situational tactical exercise
SWS	Sniper weapon system
T/O	Table of organization
TRUEX	Training in urban environment exercise
WMD	Weapons of mass destruction

Index